THE ALMANACK OF NAVAL RAVIKANT

THE ALMANACK OF NAVAL RAVIKANT

A guide to wealth and happiness

ERIC JORGENSON

AUTHORS EQUITY

Authors Equity
1123 Broadway, Suite 1008
New York, New York 10010

Cover design by Lauren Michelle Smith and Erin Tyler
Production design by Scribe Media
Illustrations by Jack Butcher

First published in 2020 by Magrathea Publishing
Second edition published in 2025 by Authors Equity

This book has been created as a public service. It is available for free download in pdf and e-reader versions on Navalmanack.com. Naval is not earning any money on this book. Naval has essays, podcasts and more at Nav.al and is on Twitter @Naval.

Library of Congress Control Number: 2025939679
Hardcover ISBN 9798893310948
Paperback ISBN 9798893310993
Ebook ISBN 9798893310962

Printed and bound in Australia by Griffin Press
First Printing

www.authorsequity.com

FOR MY PARENTS, WHO GAVE ME EVERYTHING AND ALWAYS SEEM TO FIND A WAY TO GIVE MORE.

I CONTENTS

IMPORTANT NOTES ON THIS BOOK (DISCLAIMER)

I built the Navalmanack entirely out of transcripts, Tweets, and talks Naval has shared. Every attempt is made to present Naval in his own words. However, there are a few important points.

→ The transcripts have been edited for clarity and brevity (multiple times).
→ Not all sources are primary (some excerpts are from other writers quoting Naval).
→ I can't be 100 percent certain of every source's authenticity.
→ Concepts and interpretations change over time, medium, and context.
→ Please verify phrasing with a primary source before citing Naval from this text.
→ **Please interpret generously.**

By definition, everything in this book is taken out of context. Interpretations will change over time. Read and interpret generously. Understand the original intent may be different than your interpretation in a different time, medium, format, and context.

In the process of creating this book, I may have mistakenly re-contextualized, misinterpreted, or misunderstood things. As content passed through time, space, and medium, some phrasing may have shifted in flight. Every effort has been made to maintain the original intent, but errors are (very) possible.

Interviews have been transcribed, edited, rearranged, and re-edited for readability. I did my best to keep Naval's ideas in his own words.

All brilliance in this book is Naval's; any mistakes are mine.

TWEETS AND TWEETSTORMS

Tweets are formatted like pull quotes but are unique content. I use them to summarize or punctuate an idea from the main prose.

> This formatting shows I'm quoting a tweet.

Tweetstorms are connected tweets, formatted like this:

> This is the first tweet in a tweetstorm.
>
> ↓
>
> This is the second tweet. Tweetstorms are longer series of tweets all threaded together, similar to a blog post.

BOLDED QUESTIONS

Many excerpts are from interviews by fantastic creators like Shane Parrish, Sarah Lacy, Joe Rogan, and Tim Ferriss. The questions are bolded. For simplicity and continuity, I do not distinguish various interviewers from each other.

NON-NARRATIVE

This is a choose-your-own adventure book. Jump to anything that interests you and skip anything that doesn't.

LOOK IT UP

If you find a word or concept you're not familiar with, look it up. Or, read on to find more context. Some referenced ideas are expanded upon later in the book.

CITATIONS

I've done my best to maintain context for smooth reading. Sources are in the appendix for reference. Some sources appear many times and do not appear in order.

I FOREWORD

BY TIM FERRISS

Dear Reader,

It feels strange for me to write these words, as I committed many years ago to never write forewords.

I'm making a rare exception in this case for three reasons. First, a free version of this book is being offered to the world in a digital/Kindle/eBook format with no strings attached. Second, I've known Naval for more than a decade and have long wanted someone to compile this book. Third, I'm increasing the likelihood of Naval's next child being named "Tim" (I'll settle for "Timbo," if he prefers).

Naval is one of the smartest people I've ever met, and he's also one of the most courageous. Not in the "run into the fire without thinking twice" sense, but in the "think twice and then tell everyone they're focusing on the wrong fire" sense. He is rarely part of any consensus, and the uniqueness of his life, lifestyle, family dynamics, and startup successes is a reflection of conscious choices he's made to do things differently.

He can be as blunt as a foot to the face, but that's part of what I love and respect about him: you never have to guess what Naval is thinking. I've never had to guess how he's feeling about me, someone else, or a situation. This is a huge relief in a world of double-talk and ambiguity.

We've shared a lot of meals, shared a lot of deals, and hopped around the world together. That's all to say that, while I consider myself a good people-watcher, I consider myself an excellent Naval-watcher. He is one of the people I call most for advice, and I've watched him in many habitats through many seasons: easy times, hard times, recessions, booms—you name it.

Sure, he's the CEO and a co-founder of AngelList. Sure, he previously co-founded Vast.com and Epinions, which went public as part of Shopping.com. Sure, he's an angel investor and has invested in many mega successes, including Twitter, Uber, Yammer, and OpenDNS, to name but a few.

That's all great, of course, and it shows Naval is a world-class operator instead of an armchair philosopher.

But I don't take his perspectives, maxims, and thoughts seriously because of the business stuff. There are lots of miserable "successful" people out there. Be careful about modeling those, as you will get all the bathwater with the baby.

I take Naval seriously because he:

- → Questions nearly everything
- → Can think from first principles
- → Tests things well

- → Is good at not fooling himself
- → Changes his mind regularly
- → Laughs a lot
- → Thinks holistically
- → Thinks long-term
- → And...doesn't take himself too goddamn seriously.

That last one is important.

This book will give you a good taste of what that cocktail of bullets looks like in Naval's head.

So, pay attention...but don't simply parrot his words. Follow his advice...but only if it holds up after scrutiny and stress-testing in your own life. Consider everything...but take nothing as gospel. Naval would want you to challenge him, as long as you bring your A-game.

Naval has changed my life for the better, and if you approach the following pages like a friendly but highly competent sparring partner, he might just change yours.

Keep your hands up and your mind open.

Pura Vida,
Tim Ferriss
Austin, Texas

ERIC'S NOTE (ABOUT THIS BOOK)

Throughout his career, Naval has generously shared his wisdom, and millions of people around the world follow his advice on building wealth and living happily.

Naval Ravikant is an icon in Silicon Valley and startup culture around the world. He founded multiple successful companies (Epinions during the 2000 dot-com crash, AngelList in 2010). Naval is also an angel investor, betting early on companies like Uber, Twitter, Postmates, and hundreds more.

More than a financial success, Naval has been sharing his own philosophy of life and happiness, attracting readers and listeners throughout the world. Naval is broadly followed because he is a rare combination of successful and happy. After a lifetime of study and application of philosophy, economics, and wealth creation, he has proven the impact of his principles.

Today, Naval continues to build and invest in companies almost casually, in his own artistic way, while maintaining a healthy, peaceful, and balanced life. This book collects and organizes the pieces of wisdom he has shared and shows you how to achieve the same for yourself.

Naval's life story is instructive. An introspective founder, self-taught investor, capitalist, and engineer certainly has something to teach us all.

As a first-principles thinker with no fear of speaking his truth, Naval's thoughts are often unique and thought-provoking. His instinct for seeing through life's veneer has changed how I see the world.

I've learned an enormous amount from Naval. Reading, listening, and applying his principles of wealth and happiness has given me calm confidence on my path and taught me to enjoy every moment of this journey. Closely studying his career has shown me how great things are accomplished through small, persistent steps, and how large an impact one individual can have.

I refer to his work often and recommend it to friends. Those conversations inspired me to create this book, so people can learn from his perspective whether they're new to Naval's ideas or have followed him the past ten years.

This book collects the wisdom shared by Naval over the past decade in his own words through Twitter, blog posts, and podcasts. With this book, you can get the benefits of a lifetime in a few hours.

I created this book as a public service. Tweets, podcasts, and interviews quickly get buried and lost. Knowledge this valuable deserves a more permanent, accessible format. That is my mission with this book.

I hope this acts as an introduction to Naval's ideas. I've collected his most powerful and useful ideas in his own words, woven them into a readable thread, and organized those into sections for easy reference.

I often find myself reviewing sections of this book before making an investment or opening to the Happiness chapter if I'm feeling off. Creating this book has changed me. I feel more clarity, confidence, and peace through all aspects of life. I hope reading it will do the same for you.

The Almanack is intended as a guide to be read and consulted for specific topics. If Naval doesn't answer your emails, I hope this book gives you the next-best advice.

In the first few years of publication, this book has sold more than one million copies worldwide. It has been deeply rewarding to see these ideas spread as a word-of-mouth phenomenon and hear how they have changed people's lives.

To get more useful ideas and ways to apply them to your life, visit Navalmanack.com and join my weekly email newsletter at EJorgenson.com.

Thank you for reading,
Eric

TIMELINE OF NAVAL RAVIKANT

- 1974 - Born in Delhi, India
- 1985 - Age 11 - Moved from New Delhi to Queens, NY
- 1989 - Age 14 - Attended Stuyvesant High School
- 1995 - Age 21 - Graduated Dartmouth (studied computer science and economics)
- 1999 - Age 25 - Founder/CEO of Epinions
- 2001 - Age 27 - Venture Partner at August Capital
- 2003 - Age 29 - Founder of Vast.com, a classified ad marketplace
- 2005 - Age 30 - Is called "Radioactive Mud" in Silicon Valley
- 2007 - Age 32 - Founded Hit Forge, a small VC fund originally conceived as an incubator
- 2007 - Age 32 - Launched VentureHacks blog
- 2010 - Age 34 - Launched AngelList
- 2010 - Age 34 - Invested in Uber
- 2012 - Age 36 - Lobbied Congress to get the JOBS Act passed
- 2018 - Age 43 - Is named "Angel Investor of the Year"

NOW, HERE IS NAVAL IN HIS OWN WORDS...

BACKGROUND

I grew up in a single-parent household with my mom working, going to school, and raising my brother and me as latchkey kids. We were very self-sufficient from a very early age. There was a lot of hardship, but everyone goes through hardship. It did help me in a number of ways.

We were poor immigrants. My dad came to the US—he was a pharmacist in India. But his degree wasn't accepted here, so he worked in a hardware store. Not a great upbringing, you know. My family split up.

My mother uniquely provided, against the background of hardship, unconditional and unfailing love. If you have nothing in your life, but you have at least one person that loves you unconditionally, it'll do wonders for your self-esteem.

We were in a part of New York City that isn't very safe. Basically, the library was my after-school center. After I came back from school, I would just go straight to the library and hang out there until they closed. Then, I would come home. That was my daily routine.

We moved to the US when we were very young. I didn't have many friends, so I wasn't very confident. I spent a lot of time reading. My only real friends were books. Books make for great friends, because the best thinkers of the last few thousand years tell you their nuggets of wisdom.

My first job was with an illegal catering company in the back of a van delivering Indian food when I was fifteen. Even when I was younger, I had a paper route and I washed dishes in the cafeteria.

I was a totally unknown kid in New York City from a nothing family, an "immigrants trying to survive" situation. Then, I passed the test to get into Stuyvesant High School. That saved my life, because once I had the Stuyvesant brand, I got into an Ivy League college, which led me into tech. Stuyvesant is one of those intelligence lottery situations where you can break in with instant validation. You go from being blue collar to white collar in one move.

At Dartmouth, I studied economics and computer science. There was a time when I thought I was going to be a PhD in economics.

Today, I'm an investor, personally, in about two hundred companies. Advisor to a bunch. I'm on a bunch of boards. I'm also a small partner in a cryptocurrency fund because I'm really into the potential of cryptocurrencies. I'm always cooking up something new. I always have a bunch of side projects.

All that, of course, in addition to being the founder and chairman of AngelList.

I was born poor and miserable. I'm now pretty well-off, and I'm very happy. I worked at those.

I've learned a few things, and some principles. I try to lay them out in a timeless manner, where you can figure it out for yourself. Because at the end of the day, I can't quite teach anything. I can only inspire you and maybe give you a few hooks so you can remember.

> Live, on Twitter, it's Naval (applause ensues...)
>
> On May 18th, 2007

PART I

WEALTH

How to get rich without getting lucky.

I BUILDING WEALTH

> Making money is not a thing you do—it's a skill you learn.

UNDERSTAND HOW WEALTH IS CREATED

I like to think that if I lost all my money and you dropped me on a random street in any English-speaking country, within five or ten years I'd be wealthy again because it's just a skillset I've developed that anyone can develop.

It's not really about hard work. You can work in a restaurant eighty hours a week, and you're not going to get rich. Getting rich is about knowing what to do, who to do it with, and when to do it. It is much more about understanding than purely hard work. Yes, hard work matters, and you can't skimp on it. But it has to be directed in the right way.

If you don't know yet what you should work on, the most important thing is to figure it out. You should not grind at a lot of hard work until you figure out what you should be working on.

I came up with the principles in my tweetstorm (below) for myself when I was really young, around thirteen or fourteen. I've been carrying them in my head for thirty years, and I've been living them. Over time (sadly or fortunately), the thing I got really good at was looking at businesses and figuring out the point of maximum leverage to actually create wealth and capture some of that created wealth.

This is exactly what I did my famous tweetstorm about. Of course, every one of these tweets can be extrapolated into an hour's worth of conversation. The tweetstorm below is a good starting point. The tweetstorm tries to be information-dense, very concise, high-impact, and timeless. It has all the information and principles, so if you absorb these and you work hard over ten years, you'll get what you want.

How to Get Rich (Without Getting Lucky):

↓

Seek wealth, not money or status. Wealth is having assets that earn while you sleep. Money is how we transfer time and wealth. Status is your place in the social hierarchy.

↓

Understand ethical wealth creation is possible. If you secretly despise wealth, it will elude you.

↓

Ignore people playing status games. They gain status by attacking people playing wealth creation games.

↓

You're not going to get rich renting out your time. You must own equity—a piece of a business—to gain your financial freedom.

↓

You will get rich by giving society what it wants but does not yet know how to get. At scale.

↓

Pick an industry where you can play long-term games with long-term people.

↓

The internet has massively broadened the possible space of careers. Most people haven't figured this out yet.

↓

Play iterated games. All the returns in life, whether in wealth, relationships, or knowledge, come from compound interest.

↓

Pick business partners with high intelligence, energy, and, above all, integrity.

↓

Don't partner with cynics and pessimists. Their beliefs are self-fulfilling.

↓

Learn to sell. Learn to build. If you can do both, you will be unstoppable.

↓

Arm yourself with specific knowledge, accountability, and leverage.

↓

Specific knowledge is knowledge you cannot be trained for. If society can train you, it can train someone else and replace you.

↓

Specific knowledge is found by pursuing your genuine curiosity and passion rather than whatever is hot right now.

↓

Building specific knowledge will feel like play to you but will look like work to others.

↓

When specific knowledge is taught, it's through apprenticeships, not schools.

↓

Specific knowledge is often highly technical or creative. It cannot be outsourced or automated.

↓

Embrace accountability, and take business risks under your own name. Society will reward you with responsibility, equity, and leverage.

↓

"Give me a lever long enough and a place to stand, and I will move the earth."

—Archimedes

↓

Fortunes require leverage. Business leverage comes from capital, people, and products with no marginal cost of replication (code and media).

↓

Capital means money. To raise money, apply your specific knowledge with accountability and show resulting good judgment.

↓

Labor means people working for you. It's the oldest and most fought-over form of leverage. Labor leverage will impress your parents, but don't waste your life chasing it.

↓

Capital and labor are permissioned leverage. Everyone is chasing capital, but someone has to give it to you. Everyone is trying to lead, but someone has to follow you.

↓

Code and media are permissionless leverage. They're the leverage behind the newly rich. You can create software and media that works for you while you sleep.

↓

An army of robots is freely available—it's just packed in data centers for heat and space efficiency. Use it.

↓

If you can't code, write books and blogs, record videos and podcasts.

↓

Leverage is a force multiplier for your judgment.

↓

Judgment requires experience but can be built faster by learning foundational skills.

↓

There is no skill called "business." Avoid business magazines and business classes.

↓

Study microeconomics, game theory, psychology, persuasion, ethics, mathematics, and computers.

↓

Reading is faster than listening. Doing is faster than watching.

↓

You should be too busy to "do coffee" while still keeping an uncluttered calendar.

↓

Set and enforce an aspirational personal hourly rate. If fixing a problem will save less than your hourly rate, ignore it. If outsourcing a task will cost less than your hourly rate, outsource it.

↓

Work as hard as you can. Even though who you work with and what you work on are more important than how hard you work.

↓

Become the best in the world at what you do. Keep redefining what you do until this is true.

↓

There are no get-rich-quick schemes. Those are just someone else getting rich off you.

↓

Apply specific knowledge, with leverage, and eventually you will get what you deserve.

↓

When you're finally wealthy, you'll realize it wasn't what you were seeking in the first place. But that is for another day.

Summary: Productize Yourself

Your summary says "Productize yourself"—what does that mean?

"Productize" and "yourself." "Yourself" has uniqueness. "Productize" has leverage. "Yourself" has accountability. "Productize" has specific knowledge. "Yourself" also has specific knowledge in there. So all of these pieces, you can combine them into these two words.

If you're looking toward the long-term goal of getting wealthy, you should ask yourself, "Is this authentic to me? Is it myself that I am projecting?" And then, "Am I productizing it? Am I scaling it? Am I scaling with labor or with capital or with code or with media?" So it's a very handy, simple mnemonic.

This is hard. This is why I say it takes decades—I'm not saying it takes decades to execute, but the better part of a decade may be figuring out what you can uniquely provide.

What's the difference between wealth and money?

Money is how we transfer wealth. Money is social credits. It is the ability to have credits and debits of other people's time.

If I do my job right, if I create value for society, society says, "Oh, thank you. We owe you something in the future for the work you did in the past. Here's a little IOU. Let's call that money."

Wealth is the thing you want. Wealth is assets that earn while you sleep. Wealth is the factory, the robots, cranking out things. Wealth is the computer program that's running at night, serving other customers. Wealth is even money in the bank that is being reinvested into other assets, and into other businesses.

Even a house can be a form of wealth, because you can rent it out, although that's probably a lower productivity use of land than some commercial enterprise.

So, my definition of wealth is much more businesses and assets that can earn while you sleep.

> Technology democratizes consumption but consolidates production. The best person in the world at anything gets to do it for everyone.

Society will pay you for creating things it wants. But society doesn't yet know how to create those things, because if it did, they wouldn't need you. They would already be stamped out.

Almost everything in your house, in your workplace, and on the street used to be technology at one point in time. There was a time when oil was a technology that made J.D. Rockefeller rich. There was a time when cars were technology that made Henry Ford rich.

So, technology is the set of things, as Alan Kay said, that don't quite work yet [correction: Danny Hillis]. Once something works, it's no longer technology. Society always wants new things. And if you want to be wealthy, you want to figure out which one of those things you can provide for society that it does not yet know how to get but it will want and providing it is natural to you, within your skill set, and within your capabilities.

Then, you have to figure out how to scale it because if you only build one, that's not enough. You've got to build thousands, or hundreds of thousands, or millions, or billions of them so everybody can have one. Steve Jobs (and his team, of course) figured out society would want smartphones. A computer in their pocket that had all the phone capability times one hundred and was easy to use. So, they figured out how to build it, and then they figured out how to scale it.

BECOME THE BEST IN THE WORLD AT WHAT YOU DO.

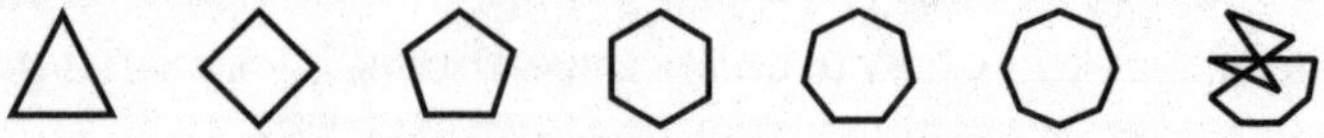

KEEP REDEFINING WHAT YOU DO UNTIL THIS IS TRUE.

FIND AND BUILD SPECIFIC KNOWLEDGE

Sales skills are a form of specific knowledge.

There's such a thing as "a natural" in sales. You run into them all the time in startups and venture capital. When you meet someone who is a natural at sales, you just know they're amazing. They're really good at what they do. That is a form of specific knowledge.

Obviously they learned somewhere, but they didn't learn it in a classroom setting. They learned probably in their childhood in the school yard, or they learned negotiating with their parents. Maybe some is a genetic component in the DNA.

But you can improve sales skills. You can read Robert Cialdini, you can go to a sales training seminar, you can do door-to-door sales. It is brutal but will train you very quickly. You can definitely improve your sales skills.

Specific knowledge cannot be taught, but it can be learned.

When I talk about specific knowledge, I mean figure out what you were doing as a kid or teenager almost effortlessly. Something you didn't even consider a skill, but people around you noticed. Your mother or your best friend growing up would know.

Examples of what your specific knowledge could be:

→ Sales skills
→ Musical talents, with the ability to pick up any instrument
→ An obsessive personality: you dive into things and remember them quickly
→ Love for science fiction: you were into reading sci-fi, which means you absorb a lot of knowledge very quickly
→ Playing a lot of games, you understand game theory pretty well
→ Gossiping, digging into your friend network. That might make you into a very interesting journalist.

The specific knowledge is sort of this weird combination of unique traits from your DNA, your unique upbringing, and your response to it. It's almost baked into your personality and your identity. Then you can hone it.

No one can compete with you on being you.

Most of life is a search for who and what needs you the most.

For example, I love to read, and I love technology. I learn very quickly, and I get bored fast. If I had gone into a profession where I was required to tunnel down for twenty years into the same topic, it wouldn't have worked. I'm in venture investing, which requires me to come up to speed very, very quickly on new technologies (and I'm rewarded for getting bored because new technologies come along). It matches up pretty well with my specific knowledge and skill sets.

I wanted to be a scientist. That is where a lot of my moral hierarchy comes from. I view scientists as being at the top of the production chain for humanity. The group of scientists who have made real breakthroughs and contributions probably added more to human society, I think, than any single other class of human beings. Not to take away anything from art or politics or engineering or business, but without science, we'd still be scrambling in the dirt fighting with sticks and trying to start fires.

> Society, business, & money are downstream of technology, which is itself downstream of science. Science applied is the engine of humanity.
>
> Corollary: Applied Scientists are the most powerful people in the world. This will be more obvious in the coming years.

My whole value system was built around scientists, and I wanted to be a great scientist. But when I actually look back at what I was uniquely good at and what I ended up spending my time doing, it was more around making money, tinkering with technology, and selling people on things. Explaining things and talking to people.

I have some sales skills, which is a form of specific knowledge. I have some analytical skills on how to make money. And I have this ability to absorb data, obsess about it, and break it down—that is a specific skill that I have. I also love tinkering with technology. And all of this stuff feels like play to me, but it looks like work to others.

There are other people to whom these things would be hard, and they say, "Well, how do I get good at being pithy and selling ideas?" Well, if you're not already good at it or if you're not really into it, maybe it's not your thing—focus on the thing that you are really into.

The first person to actually point out my real specific knowledge was my mother. She did it as an aside, talking from the kitchen, and she said it when I was fifteen or sixteen years old. I was telling a friend of mine that I want to be an astrophysicist, and she said, "No, you're going to go into business." I was like, "What, my mom's telling me I'm going to be in business? I'm going to be an astrophysicist. Mom doesn't know she's talking about." But Mom knew exactly what she was talking about.

Specific knowledge is found much more by pursuing your innate talents, your genuine curiosity, and your passion. It's not by going to school for whatever is the hottest job; it's not by going into whatever field investors say is the hottest.

Very often, specific knowledge is at the edge of knowledge. It's also stuff that's only now being figured out or is really hard to figure out. If you're not 100 percent into it, somebody else who is 100 percent into it will outperform you. And they won't just outperform you by a little bit—they'll outperform you by a lot because now we're operating the domain of ideas, compound interest really applies and leverage really applies.

> The internet has massively broadened the possible space of careers. Most people haven't figured this out yet.

You can go on the internet, and you can find your audience. And you can build a business, and create a product, and build wealth, and make people happy just uniquely expressing yourself through the internet.

The internet enables any niche interest, as long as you're the best person at it to scale out. And the great news is because every human is different, everyone is the best at something—being themselves.

Another tweet I had that is worth weaving in, but didn't go into the "How to Get Rich" tweetstorm, was very simple: "Escape competition through authenticity." Basically, when you're competing with people, it's because you're copying them. It's because you're trying to do the same thing. But every human is different. Don't copy.

If you are fundamentally building and marketing something that is an extension of who you are, no one can compete with you on that. Who's going to compete with Joe Rogan or Scott Adams? It's impossible. Is somebody else going to come along and write a better Dilbert? No. Is someone going to compete with Bill Watterson and create a better Calvin and Hobbes? No. They're being authentic.

> The best jobs are neither decreed nor degreed. They are creative expressions of continuous learners in free markets.

The most important skill for getting rich is becoming a perpetual learner. You have to know how to learn anything you want to learn. The old model of making money is going to school for four years, getting your degree, and working as a professional for thirty years. But things change fast now. Now, you have to come up to speed on a new profession within nine months, and it's obsolete four years later. But within those three productive years, you can get very wealthy.

It's much more important today to be able to become an expert in a brand-new field in nine to twelve months than to have studied the "right" thing a long time ago. You really care about having studied the foundations, so you're not scared of any book. If you go to the library and there's a book you cannot understand, you have to dig down and say, "What is the foundation required for me to learn this?" Foundations are super important.

Basic arithmetic and numeracy are way more important in life than doing calculus. Similarly, being able to convey yourself simply using ordinary English words is far more important than being able to write poetry, having an extensive vocabulary, or speaking seven different foreign languages.

Knowing how to be persuasive when speaking is far more important than being an expert digital marketer or click optimizer. Foundations are key. It's much better to be at 9/10 or 10/10 on foundations than to try and get super deep into things.

You do need to be deep in something because otherwise you'll be a mile wide and an inch deep and you won't get what you want out of life. You can only achieve mastery in one or two things. It's usually things you're obsessed about.

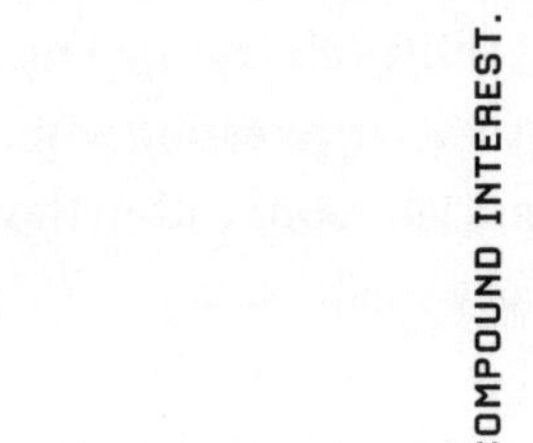

PLAY LONG-TERM GAMES WITH LONG-TERM PEOPLE

You said, "All the returns in life, whether in wealth, relationships, or knowledge, come from compound interest." How does one know if they're earning compound interest?

Compound interest is a very powerful concept. Compound interest applies to more than just compounding capital. Compounding capital is just the beginning.

Compounding in business relationships is very important. Look at some of the top roles in society, like why someone is a CEO of a public company or managing billions of dollars. It's because people trust them. They are trusted because the relationships they've built and the work they've done has compounded. They've stuck with the business and shown themselves (in a visible and accountable way) to be high-integrity people.

Compound interest also happens in your reputation. If you have a sterling reputation and you keep building it for decades upon decades, people will notice. Your reputation will literally end up being thousands or tens of thousands of times more valuable than somebody else who was very talented but is not keeping the compound interest in reputation going.

This is also true when you're working with individual people. If you've worked with somebody for five or ten years and you still enjoy working with them, obviously you trust them, and the little foibles are gone. All the normal negotiations in business relationships can work very simply because you trust each other—you know it will work out.

For example, there's another Angel in Silicon Valley named Elad Gil who I like to do deals with.

I love working with Elad because I know when the deal is being done, he will bend over backward to give me extra. He will always round off in my favor if there's an extra dollar being delivered here or there. If there's some cost to pay, he will pay it out of his own pocket, and he won't even mention it to me. Because he goes so far out of his way to treat me so well, I send him every deal I have—I try to include him in everything. Then, I go out of my way to try and pay for him. Compounding in those relationships is very valuable.

> Intentions don't matter. Actions do. That's why being ethical is hard.

When you find the right thing to do, when you find the right people to work with, invest deeply. Sticking with it for decades is really how you make the big returns in your relationships and in your money. So, compound interest is very important.

> 99% of effort is wasted.

Obviously, nothing is ever completely wasted because it's all a learning moment. You can learn from anything. But for example, when you go back to school, 99 percent of the term papers you did, books you read, exercises you did, things you learned, they don't really apply. You might have read geography and history you never reuse. You might have studied a language you don't speak anymore. You might have studied a branch of mathematics you completely forgot.

Of course, these are learning experiences. You did learn. You learned the value of hard work; you might have learned something that went deep into your psyche and became a piece of what you're doing now. But at least when it comes to the goal-oriented life, only about 1 percent of the efforts you made paid off.

Another example is all the people you dated until you met your husband or wife. It was wasted time in the goal sense. Not wasted in the exponential sense, not wasted in the learning sense, but definitely wasted in the goal sense.

The reason I say this is not to make some glib comment about how 99 percent of your life is wasted and only 1 percent is useful. I say this because you should be very thoughtful and realize in most things (relationships, work, even in learning) what you're trying to do is find the thing you can go all-in on to earn compound interest.

When you're dating, the instant you know this relationship is not going to be the one that leads to marriage, you should probably move on. When you're studying something, like a geography or history class, and you realize you are never going to use the information, drop the class. It's a waste of time. It's a waste of your brain energy.

I'm not saying don't do the 99 percent, because it's very hard to identify what the 1 percent is. What I'm saying is: when you find the 1 percent of your discipline which will not be wasted, which you'll be able to invest in for the rest of your life and has meaning to you—go all-in and forget about the rest.

INTENTIONS DON'T MATTER.

ACTIONS DO.

TAKE ON ACCOUNTABILITY

> Embrace accountability and take business risks under your own name. Society will reward you with responsibility, equity, and leverage.

To get rich, you need leverage. Leverage comes in labor, comes in capital, or it can come through code or media. But most of these, like labor and capital, people have to give to you. For labor, somebody has to follow you. For capital, somebody has to give you money, assets to manage, or machines.

So to get these things, you have to build credibility, and you have to do it under your own name as much as possible, which is risky. So, accountability is a double-edged thing. It allows you to take credit when things go well and to bear the brunt of the failure when things go badly.

Clear accountability is important. Without accountability, you don't have incentives. Without accountability, you can't build credibility. But you take risks. You risk failure. You risk humiliation. You risk failure under your own name.

Luckily, in modern society, there's no more debtors' prison and people aren't imprisoned or executed for losing other people's money, but we're still socially hardwired to not fail in public under our own names. The people who have the ability to fail in public under their own names actually gain a lot of power.

I'll give a personal anecdote. Up until about 2013, 2014, my public persona was entirely around startups and investing. Only around 2014, 2015 did I start talking about philosophy and psychological things and broader things. It made me a little nervous because I was doing it under my own name. There were definitely people in the industry who sent me messages through the backchannel like, "What are you doing? You're ending your career. This is stupid."

I kind of just went with it. I took a risk. Same with crypto. Early on, I took a risk. But when you put your name out there, you take a risk with certain things. You also get to reap the rewards. You get the benefits.

In the old days, the captain was expected to go down with the ship. If the ship was sinking, then literally the last person to get off was the captain. Accountability does come with real risks, but we're talking about a business context.

The risk here would be you would probably be the last one to get your capital back out. You'd be the last one to get paid for your time. The time that you put in, the capital you put into the company, these are at risk.

Realize that in modern society, the downside risk is not that large. Even personal bankruptcy can wipe the debts clean in good ecosystems. I'm most familiar with Silicon Valley, but generally, people will forgive failures as long as you were honest and made a high-integrity effort.

There's not really that much to fear in terms of failure, and so people should take on a lot more accountability than they do.

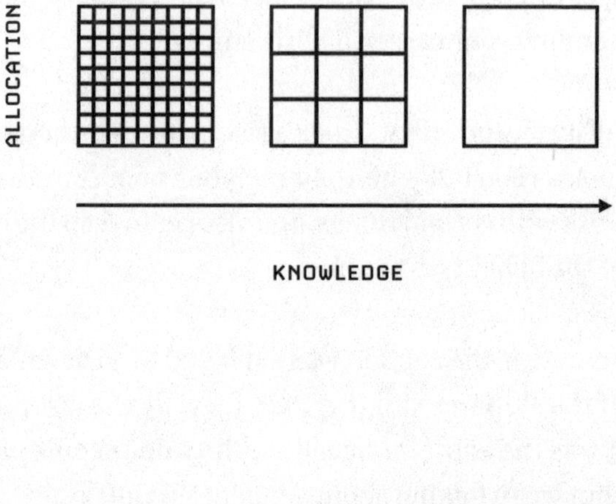

BUILD OR BUY EQUITY IN A BUSINESS

> If you don't own a piece of a business, you don't have a path towards financial freedom.

Why is owning equity in a business important to becoming rich?

It's ownership versus wage work. If you are paid for renting out your time, even lawyers and doctors, you can make some money, but you're not going to make the money that gives you financial freedom. You're not going to have passive income where a business is earning for you while you are on vacation.

This is probably one of the most important points. People seem to think you can create wealth—make money through work. It's probably not going to work. There are many reasons for that.

Without ownership, your inputs are very closely tied to your outputs. In almost any salaried job, even one paying a lot per hour like a lawyer or a doctor, you're still putting in the hours, and every hour you get paid.

Without ownership, when you're sleeping, you're not earning. When you're retired, you're not earning. When you're on vacation, you're not earning. And you can't earn nonlinearly.

If you look at even doctors who get rich (like really rich), it's because they open a business. They open a private practice. The private practice builds a brand, and the brand attracts people. Or they build some kind of a medical device, a procedure, or a process with an intellectual property.

Essentially, you're working for somebody else, and that person is taking on the risk and has the accountability, the intellectual property, and the brand. They're not going to pay you enough. They're going to pay you the bare minimum they have to, to get you to do their job. That can be a high bare minimum, but it's still not going to be true wealth where you're retired but still earning.

Owning equity in a company basically means you own the upside. When you own debt, you own guaranteed revenue streams and you own the downside. You want to own equity. If you don't own equity in a business, your odds of making money are very slim.

You have to work up to the point where you can own equity in a business. You could own equity as a small shareholder where you bought stock. You could also own it as an owner where you started the company. Ownership is really important.

Everybody who really makes money at some point owns a piece of a product, a business, or some IP. That can be through stock options if you work at a tech company. That's a fine way to start.

But usually, the real wealth is created by starting your own companies or even by investing. In an investment firm, they're buying equity. These are the routes to wealth. It doesn't come through the hours.

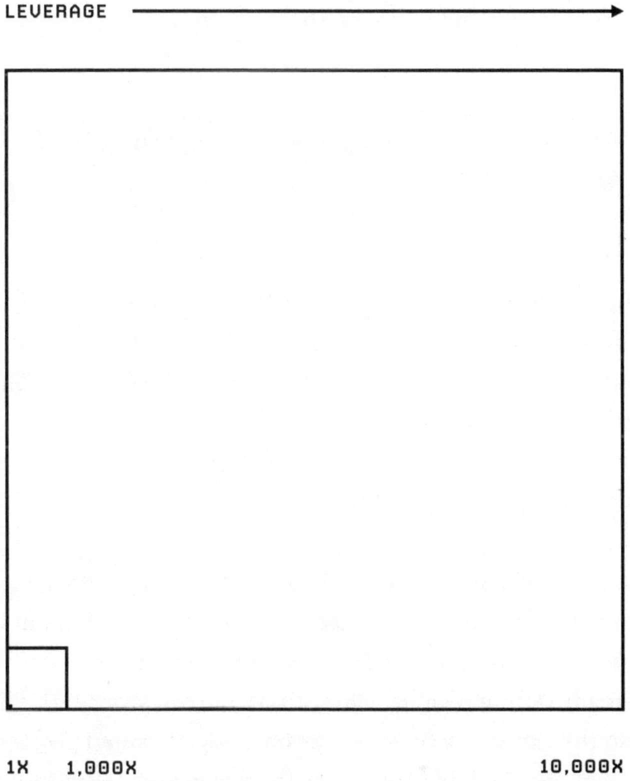

FIND A POSITION OF LEVERAGE

We live in an age of infinite leverage, and the economic rewards for genuine intellectual curiosity have never been higher. Following your genuine intellectual curiosity is a better foundation for a career than following whatever is making money right now.

Knowledge only you know or only a small set of people knows is going to come out of your passions and your hobbies, oddly enough. If you have hobbies around your intellectual curiosity, you're more likely to develop these passions.

> If it entertains you now but will bore you someday, it's a distraction. Keep looking.

I only really want to do things for their own sake. That is one definition of art. Whether it's business, exercise, romance, friendship, whatever, I think the meaning of life is to do things for their own sake. Ironically, when you do things for their own sake, you create your best work. Even if you're just trying to make money, you will actually be the most successful.

The year I generated the most wealth for myself was actually the year I worked the least hard and cared the least about the future. I was mostly doing things for the sheer fun of it. I was basically telling people, "I'm retired, I'm not working." Then, I had the time for whatever was my highest valued project in front of me. By doing things for their own sake, I did them at their best.

The less you want something, the less you're thinking about it, the less you're obsessing over it, the more you're going to do it in a natural way. The more you're going to do it for yourself. You're going to do it in a way you're good at, and you're going to stick with it. The people around you will see the quality of your work is higher.

Follow your intellectual curiosity more than whatever is "hot" right now. If your curiosity ever leads you to a place where society eventually wants to go, you'll get paid extremely well.

You're more likely to have skills society does not yet know how to train other people to do. If someone can train other people how to do something, then they can replace you. If they can replace you, then they don't have to pay you a lot. You want to know how to do something other people don't know how to do at the time period when those skills are in demand.

> If they can train you to do it, then eventually they will train a computer to do it.

You get rewarded by society for giving it what it wants and doesn't know how to get elsewhere. A lot of people think you can go to school and study for how to make money, but the reality is, there's no skill called "business."

Think about what product or service society wants but does not yet know how to get. You want to become the person who delivers it and delivers it at scale. That is really the challenge of how to make money.

> Now, the problem is becoming good at whatever "it" is. It moves around from generation to generation, but a lot of it happens to be in technology.

You are waiting for your moment when something emerges in the world, they need a skill set, and you're uniquely qualified. You build your brand in the meantime on Twitter, on YouTube, and by giving away free work. You make a name for yourself, and you take some risk in the process. When it is time to move on the opportunity, you can do so with leverage—the maximum leverage possible.

There are three broad classes of leverage:

One form of leverage is labor—other humans working for you. It is the oldest form of leverage, and actually not a great one in the modern world. I would argue this is the worst form of leverage that you could possibly use. Managing other people is incredibly messy. It requires tremendous leadership skills. You're one short hop from a mutiny or getting eaten or torn apart by the mob.

Money is good as a form of leverage. It means every time you make a decision, you multiply it with money. Capital is a trickier form of leverage to use. It's more modern. It's the one that people have used to get fabulously wealthy in the last century. It's probably been the dominant form of leverage in the last century.

You can see this by looking for the richest people. It's bankers, politicians in corrupt countries who print money, essentially people who move large amounts of money around. If you look at the top of very large companies, outside of technology companies, in many, many large old companies, the CEO job is really a financial job.

It scales very, very well. If you get good at managing capital, you can manage more and more capital much more easily than you can manage more and more people.

The final form of leverage is brand new—the most democratic form. It is: "**products with no marginal cost of replica-**

tion." This includes books, media, movies, and code. Code is probably the most powerful form of permissionless leverage. All you need is a computer—you don't need anyone's permission.

> Forget rich versus poor, white-collar versus blue. It's now leveraged versus un-leveraged.

The most interesting and the most important form of leverage is the idea of products that have no marginal cost of replication. This is the new form of leverage. This was only invented in the last few hundred years. It started with the printing press. It accelerated with broadcast media, and now it's really blown up with the internet and with coding. Now, you can multiply your efforts without involving other humans and without needing money from other humans.

This book is a form of leverage. Long ago, I would have had to sit in a lecture hall and lecture each of you personally. I would have maybe reached a few hundred people, and that would have been that.

This newest form of leverage is where all the new fortunes are made, all the new billionaires. For the last generation, fortunes were made by capital. The people who made fortunes were the Warren Buffetts of the world.

But the new generation's fortunes are all made through code or media. Joe Rogan making $50 million to $100 million a year from his podcast. You're going to have PewDiePie. I don't know how much money he's rolling in, but he's bigger than the news.

And of course, there's Jeff Bezos, Mark Zuckerberg, Larry Page, Sergey Brin, Bill Gates, and Steve Jobs. Their wealth is all code-based leverage.

Probably the most interesting thing to keep in mind about new forms of leverage is they are permissionless. They don't require somebody else's permission for you to use them or succeed. For labor leverage, somebody has to decide to follow you. For capital leverage, somebody has to give you money to invest or to turn into a product.

Coding, writing books, recording podcasts, tweeting, YouTubing—these kinds of things are permissionless. You don't need anyone's permission to do them, and that's why they are very egalitarian. They're great equalizers of leverage. Every great software developer, for example, now has an army of robots working for him at nighttime while he or she sleeps, after they've written the code, and it's cranking away.

> You're never going to get rich renting out your time.

Whenever you can in life, optimize for independence rather than pay. If you have independence and you're accountable on your output, as opposed to your input—that's the dream.

Humans evolved in societies where there was no leverage. If I was chopping wood or carrying water for you, you knew eight hours put in would be equal to about eight hours of output. Now we've invented leverage—through capital, cooperation, technology, productivity, all these means. We live in an age of leverage. As a worker, you want to be as leveraged as possible so you have a huge impact without as much time or physical effort.

A leveraged worker can out-produce a non-leveraged worker by a factor of one thousand or ten thousand. With a leveraged worker, judgment is far more important than how much time they put in or how hard they work.

> Forget 10x programmers. 1,000x programmers really exist, we just don't fully acknowledge it. See @ID_AA_Carmack, @notch, Satoshi Nakamoto, etc.

For example, a good software engineer, just by writing the right little piece of code and creating the right little application, can literally create half a billion dollars' worth of value for a company. But ten engineers working ten times as hard, just because they choose the wrong model, the wrong product, wrote it the wrong way, or put in the wrong viral loop, have basically wasted their time. Inputs don't match outputs, especially for leveraged workers.

What you want in life is to be in control of your time. You want to get into a leveraged job where you control your own time and you're tracked on the outputs. If you do something incredible to move the needle on the business, they have to pay you. Especially if they don't know how you did it because it's innate to your obsession or your skill or your innate abilities, they're going to have to keep paying you to do it.

If you have specific knowledge, you have accountability and you have leverage; they have to pay you what you're worth. If they pay you what you're worth, then you can get your time back—you can be hyper-efficient. You're not doing meetings for meetings' sake, you're not trying to impress other people, you're not writing things down to make it look like you did work. All you care about is the actual work itself.

When you do just the actual work itself, you'll be far more productive, far more efficient. You'll work when you feel like it—when you're high-energy—and you won't be trying to struggle through when you're low energy. You'll gain your time back.

> Forty hour work weeks are a relic of the Industrial Age. Knowledge workers function like athletes—train and sprint, then rest and reassess.

Sales is an example—especially very high-end sales. If you're a real estate agent out there selling houses, it's not a great job, necessarily. It's very crowded. But if you're a top-tier real estate agent, you know how to market yourself and you know how to sell houses, it's possible you could sell $5 million mansions in one tenth of the time while somebody else is struggling to sell $100,000 apartments or condos. Real estate agent is a job with input and output disconnected.

Building any product and selling any product fits this description. And fundamentally, what else is there? Where you don't necessarily want to be is a support role, like customer service. In customer service, unfortunately, inputs and outputs relate relatively close to each other, and the hours you put in matter.

Tools and leverage create this disconnection between inputs and outputs. The higher the creativity component of a profession, the more likely it is to have disconnected inputs and outputs. If you're looking at professions where your inputs and your outputs are highly connected, it's going to be very hard to create wealth and make wealth for yourself in that process.

> If you want to be part of a great tech company, then you need to be able to SELL or BUILD. If you don't do either, learn.

Learn to sell, learn to build. If you can do both, you will be unstoppable.

These are two very broad categories. One is building the product. This is hard, and it's multivariate. It can include design; it can include development; it can include manufacturing, logistics, procurement; and it can even be designing and operating a service. It has many, many definitions.

But in every industry, there is a definition of the builder. In our tech industry, it's the CTO, it's the programmer, it's the software engineer or hardware engineer. But even in the laundry business, it could be the person who's building the laundry service, who is making the trains run on time, who's making sure all the clothes end up in the right place at the right time, and so on.

The other side of it is sales. Again, selling has a very broad definition. Selling doesn't necessarily just mean selling to individual customers, but it can mean marketing, it can mean communicating, it can mean recruiting, it can mean raising money, it can mean inspiring people, it could mean doing PR. It's a broad umbrella category.

> Earn with your mind, not your time.

Let's talk more about the real estate business. The worst kind of job is someone who's doing labor to repair a house. Maybe you get paid ten dollars or twenty dollars an hour. You go to people's houses, your boss demands you're there at 8:00 a.m., and you repair your piece of the house. Here, you have zero leverage. You have some accountability, but not really, because your accountability is to your boss, not to the client. You don't have any real specific knowledge, since what you're doing is labor lots of people can do. You're not going to get paid a lot. You're getting paid minimum wage plus a little bit for your skill and your time.

The next level up might be the general contractor working on the house for the owner. They may be getting paid $50,000 to do the whole project, then they're paying the labor fifteen dollars an hour and they're keeping the difference.

A general contractor is obviously a better place to be. But how do we measure it? How do we know it's better? Well, we know it's better because this person has some accountability. They're responsible for the outcome, they have to sweat at night if things aren't working. Contractors have leverage through laborers working for them. They also have little bit more specific knowledge: how to organize a team, make them show up on time, and how to deal with city regulations.

The next level up might be a real estate developer. A developer is someone who's going to buy a property, hire a bunch of contractors, and transform it into something higher value. They probably have to take out a loan to buy a house or go to investors to raise money. They buy the old house, tear it down, rebuild it, and sell it. Instead of $50,000 like the general contractor, or fifteen dollars an hour like the laborer, the developer might be able to make a million dollars or half a million dollars in profit when they sell the house for more than they bought it for, including the expenses of construction. But now, notice what is required from the developer: a very high level of accountability.

The developer takes on more risk, more accountability, has more leverage, and needs to have more specific knowledge. They need to understand fundraising, city regulations, where the real estate market is headed, and whether they should take the risk or not. It is more difficult.

The next level up might be someone who's managing money in a real estate fund. They have an enormous amount of capital leverage. They're dealing with lots and lots of developers, and they're buying huge amounts of housing inventory.

One level beyond that might be somebody who says, "Actually, I want to bring the maximum leverage to bear in this market and the maximum specific knowledge." That person would say, "Well, I understand real estate, and I understand everything from basic housing construction, to building properties and selling them, to how real estate markets move and thrive, and I also understand the technology business. I understand how to recruit developers, how to write code, and how to build a good product, and I understand how to raise money from venture capitalists, how to return it, and how all of that works."

Obviously, not a single person may know this. You may pull a team together to do it where each have different skill sets, but that combined entity would have specific knowledge in technology and in real estate. It would have massive accountability because that company's name would be a very high-risk, high-reward effort attached to the whole thing, and people would devote their lives to it and take on significant risk. It would have leverage in code with lots of developers. It would have capital with investors putting money in and the founder's own capital. It would have some of the highest-quality labor you can find, which is high-quality engineers, designers, and marketers who are working on the company.

Then, you may end up with a Trulia, Redfin, or Zillow company, and then the upside could potentially be in the billions of dollars, or the hundreds of millions of dollars.

Each level has increasing leverage, increasing accountability, increasingly specific knowledge. You're adding in money-based leverage on top of labor-based leverage. Adding in code-based leverage on top of money and labor allows you to actually create something bigger and bigger and get closer and closer to owning all the upside, not just being paid a salary.

You start as a salaried employee. But you want to work your way up to try and get higher leverage, more accountability, and specific knowledge. The combination of those over a long period of time with the magic of compound interest will make you wealthy.

The one thing you have to avoid is the risk of ruin.

Avoiding ruin means stay out of jail. So, don't do anything illegal. It's never worth it to wear an orange jumpsuit. Stay out of total catastrophic loss. Avoiding ruin could also mean you stay out of things that could be physically dangerous or hurt your body. You have to watch your health.

Stay out of things that could cause you to lose all of your capital, all of your savings. Don't gamble everything on one go. Instead, take rationally optimistic bets with big upsides.

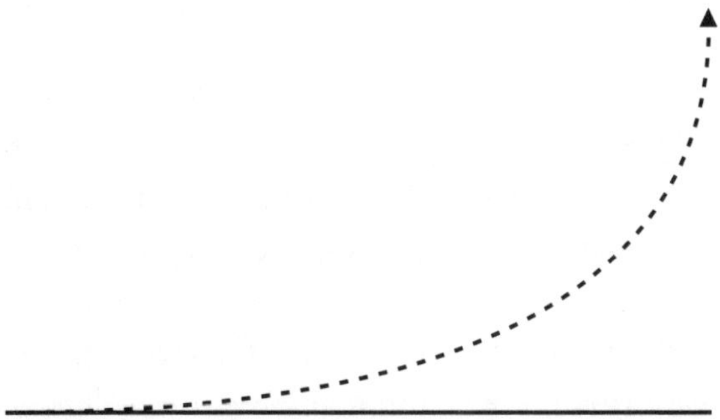

EARN WITH YOUR MIND,

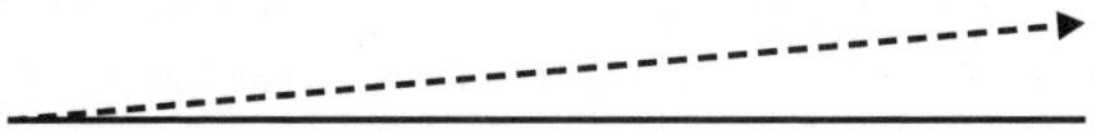

NOT YOUR TIME.

GET PAID FOR YOUR JUDGMENT

Choosing what kinds of jobs, careers, or fields you get into and what sort of deals you're willing to take from your employer will give you much more free time. Then, you don't have to worry as much about time management. I would love to be paid purely for my judgment, not for any work. I want a robot, capital, or computer to do the work, but I want to be paid for my judgment.

I think every human should aspire to being knowledgeable about certain things and being paid for our unique knowledge. We have as much leverage as is possible in our business, whether it's through robots or computers or what have you. Then, we can be masters of our own time because we are just being tracked on outputs and not inputs.

Imagine someone comes along who demonstrably has slightly better judgment. They're right 85 percent of the time instead of 75 percent. You will pay them $50 million, $100 million, $200 million, whatever it takes, because 10 percent better judgment steering a $100 billion ship is very valuable. CEOs are highly paid because of their leverage. Small differences in judgment and capability really get amplified.

Demonstrated judgment—credibility around the judgment—is so critical. Warren Buffett wins here because he has massive credibility. He's been highly accountable. He's been right over and over in the public domain. He's built a reputation for very high integrity, so you can trust him. People will throw infinite leverage behind him because of his judgment. Nobody asks him how hard he works. Nobody asks him when he wakes up or when he goes to sleep. They're like, "Warren, just do your thing."

Judgment—especially demonstrated judgment, with high accountability and a clear track record—is critical.

> We waste our time with short-term thinking and busywork. Warren Buffett spends a year deciding and a day acting. That act lasts decades.

Just from being marginally better, like running a quarter mile a fraction of a second faster, some people get paid a lot more—orders of magnitude more. Leverage magnifies those differences even more. Being at the extreme in your art is very important in the age of leverage.

SOLVE VIA ITERATION.

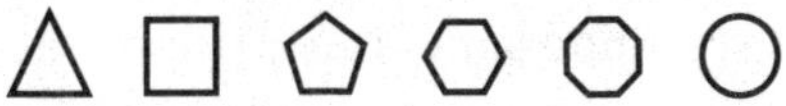

THEN GET PAID VIA REPETITION.

PRIORITIZE AND FOCUS

I've encountered plenty of bad luck along the way. The first little fortune I made I instantly lost in the stock market. The second little fortune I made, or should have made, I basically got cheated out of by my business partners. It's only the third time around that has been a charm.

Even then, it has been a slow and steady struggle. I haven't made money in my life in one giant payout. It has always been a whole bunch of small things piling up. It's more about consistently creating wealth by creating businesses, creating opportunities, and creating investments. It hasn't been a giant one-off thing. My personal wealth has not been generated by one big year. It just stacks up a little bit, a few chips at a time: more options, more businesses, more investments, more things I can do.

Thanks to the internet, opportunities are massively abundant. In fact, I have too many ways to make money. I don't have enough time. I literally have opportunities pouring out of my ears, and I keep running out of time. There are so many ways to create wealth, to create products, to create businesses, and to get paid by society as a byproduct. I just can't handle them all.

> Value your time at an hourly rate, and ruthlessly spend to save time at that rate. You will never be worth more than you think you're worth.

No one is going to value you more than you value yourself. You just have to set a very high personal hourly rate and you have to stick to it. Even when I was young, I just decided I was worth a lot more than the market thought I was worth, and I started treating myself that way.

Always factor your time into every decision. How much time does it take? It's going to take you an hour to get across town to get something. If you value yourself at one hundred dollars an hour, that's basically throwing one hundred dollars out of your pocket. Are you going to do that?

Fast-forward to your wealthy self and pick some intermediate hourly rate. For me, believe it or not, back when you could have hired me...Which now obviously you can't, but back when you could have hired me...this was true a decade ago or even two decades ago, before I had any real money. My hourly rate, I used to say to myself over and over, is $5,000 an hour. Today when I look back, really it was about $1,000 an hour.

Of course, I still ended up doing stupid things like arguing with the electrician or returning the broken speaker, but I shouldn't have, and I did a lot less than any of my friends would. I would make a theatrical show out of throwing something in the trash pile or giving it to Salvation Army rather than trying to return it or handing something to people rather than trying to fix it.

I would argue with my girlfriends, and even today it's my wife, "I don't do that. That's not a problem that I solve." I still argue that with my mother when she hands me little to-do's. I just don't do that. I would rather hire you an assistant. This was true even when I didn't have money.

Another way of thinking about something is, if you can outsource something or not do something for less than your hourly rate, outsource it or don't do it. If you can hire someone to do it for less than your hourly rate, hire them. That even includes things like cooking. You may want to eat your healthy home cooked meals, but if you can outsource it, do that instead.

Set a very high hourly aspirational rate for yourself and stick to it. It should seem and feel absurdly high. If it doesn't, it's not high enough. Whatever you picked, my advice to you would be to raise it. Like I said, for myself, even before I had money, for the longest time I used $5,000 an hour. And if you extrapolate that out into what it looks like as an annual salary, it's multiple millions of dollars per year.

Ironically, I actually think I've beaten it. I'm not the hardest working person—I'm actually a lazy person. I work through bursts of energy where I'm really motivated with something. If I actually look at how much I've earned per actual hour that I've put in, it's probably quite a bit higher than that.

Can you expand on your statement, "If you secretly despise wealth, it will elude you"?

If you get into a relative mindset, you're always going to hate people who do better than you, you're always going to be jealous or envious of them. They'll sense those feelings when you try and do business with them. When you try and do business with somebody, if you have any bad thoughts or any judgments about them, they will feel it. Humans are wired to feel what the other person deep down inside feels. You have to get out of a relative mindset.

Literally, being anti-wealth will prevent you from becoming wealthy, because you will not have the right mindset for it, you won't have the right spirit, and you won't be dealing with people on the right level. Be optimistic, be positive. It's important. Optimists actually do better in the long run.

> The business world has many people playing zero sum games and a few playing positive sum games searching for each other in the crowd.

There are fundamentally two huge games in life that people play. One is the money game. Because money is not going to solve all of your problems, but it's going to solve all of your money problems. People realize that, so they want to make money.

But at the same time, many of them, deep down, believe they can't make money. They don't want any wealth creation to happen. So, they attack the whole enterprise by saying, "Well, making money is evil. You shouldn't do it."

But they're actually playing the other game, which is the status game. They're trying to be high status in the eyes of other people watching by saying, "Well, I don't need money. We don't want money." Status is your ranking in the social hierarchy.

> Wealth creation is an evolutionarily recent positive-sum game. Status is an old zero-sum game. Those attacking wealth creation are often just seeking status.

Status is a zero-sum game. It's a very old game. We've been playing it since monkey tribes. It's hierarchical. Who's number one? Who's number two? Who's number three? And for number three to move to number two, number two has to move out of that slot. So, status is a zero-sum game.

Politics is an example of a status game. Even sports are an example of a status game. To be the winner, there must be a loser. I don't fundamentally love status games. They play an important role in our society, so we can figure out who's in charge. But fundamentally, you play them because they're a necessary evil.

The problem is, to win at a status game, you have to put somebody else down. That's why you should avoid status games in your life—they make you into an angry, combative person. You're always fighting to put other people down, to put yourself and the people you like up.

Status games are always going to exist. There's no way around it, but realize most of the time, when you're trying to create wealth and you're getting attacked by someone else, they're trying to increase their own status at your expense. They're playing a different game. And it's a worse game. It's a zero-sum game instead of a positive-sum game.

> Play stupid games, win stupid prizes.

What is the most important thing to do for younger people starting out?

Spend more time making the big decisions. There are basically three really big decisions you make in your early life: where you live, who you're with, and what you do.

We spend very little time deciding which relationship to get into. We spend so much time in a job, but we spend so little time deciding which job to get into. Choosing what city to live in can almost completely determine the trajectory of your life, but we spend so little time trying to figure out what city to live in.

> Advice to a young engineer considering moving to San Francisco: "Do you want to leave your friends behind? Or be the one left behind?"

If you're going to live in a city for ten years, if you're going to be in a job for five years, if you're in a relationship for a decade, you should be spending one to two years deciding these things. These are highly dominating decisions. Those three decisions really matter.

You have to say no to everything and free up your time so you can solve the important problems. Those three are probably the three biggest ones.

What are one or two steps you'd take to surround yourself with successful people?

Figure out what you're good at, and start helping other people with it. Give it away. Pay it forward. Karma works because people are consistent. On a long enough timescale, you will attract what you project. But don't measure—your patience will run out if you count.

> An old boss once warned: "You'll never be rich since you're obviously smart, and someone will always offer you a job that's just good enough."

How did you decide to start your first company?

I was working at this tech company called @Home Network, and I told everybody around me—my boss, coworkers, my friends, "In Silicon Valley, all of these other people are starting companies. It looks like they can do it. I'm going to start a company. I'm just here temporarily. I'm an entrepreneur."

...I didn't actually mean to trick myself into it. It wasn't a deliberate, calculated thing.

I was just venting, talking out loud, being overly honest. But I didn't actually start a company. This was in 1996, it was a much scarier, more difficult proposition to start a company then. Sure enough, everyone started saying "What are you still doing here? I thought you were leaving to start a company?" and "Wow, you're still here..." I was literally embarrassed into starting my own company.

Yes, I know some people aren't necessarily ready to be entrepreneurs, but long-term, where did we come up with this idea the correct logical thing to do is for everybody to work for somebody else? It is a very hierarchical model.

FIND WORK THAT FEELS LIKE PLAY

Humans evolved as hunters and gatherers where we all worked for ourselves. It's only at the beginning of agriculture we became more hierarchical. The Industrial Revolution and factories made us extremely hierarchical because one individual couldn't necessarily own or build a factory, but now, thanks to the internet, we're going back to an age where more and more people can work for themselves. I would rather be a failed entrepreneur than someone who never tried. Because even a failed entrepreneur has the skill set to make it on their own.

> There are almost 7 billion people on this planet. Someday, I hope, there will be almost 7 billion companies.

I learned how to make money because it was a necessity. After it stopped being a necessity, I stopped caring about it. At least for me, work was a means to an end. Making money was a means to an end. I'm much more interested in solving problems than I am in making money.

Any end goal will just lead to another goal, lead to another goal. We just play games in life. When you grow up, you're playing the school game, or you're playing the social game. Then you're playing the money game, and then you're playing the status game. These games just have longer and longer and longer-lived horizons. At some point, at least I believe, these are all just games. These are games where the outcome really stops mattering once you see through the game.

Then you just get tired of games. I would say I'm at the stage where I'm just tired of games. I don't think there is any end goal or purpose. I'm just living life as I want to. I'm literally just doing it moment to moment.

I want to be off the hedonic treadmill.

What you really want is freedom. You want freedom from your money problems, right? I think that's okay. Once you can solve your money problems, either by lowering your lifestyle or by making enough money, you want to retire. Not retirement at sixty-five years old, sitting in a nursing home collecting a check retirement—it's a different definition.

What is your definition of retirement?

Retirement is when you stop sacrificing today for an imaginary tomorrow. When today is complete, in and of itself, you're retired.

How do you get there?

Well, one way is to have so much money saved that your passive income (without you lifting a finger) covers your burn rate.

A second is you just drive your burn rate down to zero—you become a monk.

A third is you're doing something you love. You enjoy it so much, it's not about the money. So there are multiple ways to retirement.

The way to get out of the competition trap is to be authentic, to find the thing you know how to do better than anybody. You know how to do it better because you love it, and no one can compete with you. If you love to do it, be authentic, and then figure out how to map that to what society actually wants. Apply some leverage and put your name on it. You take the risks, but you gain the rewards, have ownership and equity in what you're doing, and just crank it up.

Did your motivation to earn money drop after you became financially independent?

Yes and no. It did in the sense the desperation was gone.

But if anything, creating businesses and making money are now more of an "art."

> Whether in commerce, science, or politics—history remembers the artists.

Art is creativity. Art is anything done for its own sake. What are the things that are done for their own sake, and there's nothing behind them? Loving somebody, creating something, playing. To me, creating businesses is play. I create businesses because it's fun, because I'm into the product.

I can create a new business within three months: raise the money, assemble a team, and launch it. It's fun for me. It's really cool to see what can I put together. It makes money almost as a side effect. Creating businesses is the game I became good at. It's just my motivation has shifted from being goal-oriented to being artistic. Ironically, I think I'm much better at it now.

Even when I invest, it's because I like the people involved, I like hanging out with them, I learn from them, I think the product is really cool. These days, I will pass on great investments because I don't find the products interesting.

These are not 100 percent-or-nothing things. You can start moving more and more toward that goal in your life. It's a goal.

When I was younger, I used to be so desperate to make money that I would have done anything. If you'd shown up and said, "Hey, I've got a sewage trucking business, want to go into that?" I would have said, "Great, I want to make money!" Thank God no one gave me that opportunity. I'm glad I went down the road of technology and science, which I genuinely enjoy. I got to combine my vocation and my avocation.

I'm always "working." It looks like work to others, but it feels like play to me. And that's how I know no one can compete with me on it. Because I'm just playing, for sixteen hours a day. If others want to compete with me, they're going to work, and they're going to lose because they're not going to do it for sixteen hours a day, seven days a week.

What was your figure where you thought you were financially safe?

Money is not the root of all evil; there's nothing evil about it. But the lust for money is bad. The lust for money is not bad in a social sense. It's not bad in the sense of "you're a bad person for lusting for money." It's bad for you.

Lusting for money is bad for us because it is a bottomless pit. It will always occupy your mind. If you love money, and you make it, there's never enough. There is never enough because the desire is turned on and doesn't turn off at some number. It's a fallacy to think it turns off at some number.

The punishment for the love of money is delivered at the same time as the money. As you make money, you just want even more, and you become paranoid and fearful of losing what you do have. There's no free lunch.

You make money to solve your money and material problems. I think the best way to stay away from this constant love of money is to not upgrade your lifestyle as you make money. It's very easy to keep upgrading your lifestyle as you make money. But if you can hold your lifestyle fixed and hopefully make your money in giant lump sums as opposed to a trickle at a time, you won't have time to upgrade your lifestyle. You may get so far ahead you actually become financially free.

Another thing that helps: I value freedom above everything else. All kinds of freedom: freedom to do what I want, freedom from things I don't want to do, freedom from my own emotions or things that may disturb my peace. For me, freedom is my number one value.

To the extent money buys freedom, it's great. But to the extent it makes me less free, which it definitely does at some level as well, I don't like it.

> The winners of any game are the people who are so addicted they continue playing even as the marginal utility from winning declines.

Do I have to start a company to be successful?

The most successful class of people in Silicon Valley on a consistent basis are either the venture capitalists (because they are diversified and control what used to be a scarce resource) or people who are very good at identifying companies that have just hit product/market fit. Those people have the background, expertise, and references those companies really want to help them scale. Then, they go into the latest Dropbox or the latest Airbnb.

The people who were at Google, then joined Facebook when it was one hundred people, and then joined Stripe when it was one hundred people?

When Zuckerberg was just starting to scale his company and panicked, he was like, "I don't know how to do this." And he called Jim Breyer [venture capitalist and founder of Accel Partners]. And Jim Breyer said, "Well, I have this really great head of product at this other company, and you need this person." Those people tend to do the best, risk-adjusted over a long period of time, other than the venture investors themselves.

Some of the most successful people I've seen in Silicon Valley had breakouts very early in their careers. They got promoted to VP, director, or CEO, or started a company that did well fairly early. If you're not getting promoted through the ranks, it gets a lot harder to catch up later in life. It's good to be in a smaller company early because there's less of an infrastructure to prevent early promotion.

For someone who is early in their career (and maybe even later), the single most important thing about a company is the alumni network you're going to build. Think about who you will work with and what those people are going on to do.

HOW TO GET LUCKY

Why do you say, "Get rich without getting lucky"?

In 1,000 parallel universes, you want to be wealthy in 999 of them. You don't want to be wealthy in the fifty of them where you got lucky, so we want to factor luck out of it.

But getting lucky would help, right?

Just recently, Babak Nivi, my co-founder, and I were talking on Twitter about how one gets lucky, and there are really four kinds of luck we were talking about.

The first kind of luck is blind luck where one just gets lucky because something completely out of their control happened. This includes fortune, fate, etc.

Then, there's luck through persistence, hard work, hustle, and motion. This is when you're running around creating opportunities. You're generating a lot of energy, you're doing a lot to stir things up. It's almost like mixing a petri dish or mixing a bunch of reagents and seeing what combines. You're just generating enough force, hustle, and energy for luck to find you.

A third way is you become very good at spotting luck. If you are very skilled in a field, you will notice when a lucky break happens in your field, and other people who aren't attuned to it won't notice. So, you become sensitive to luck.

The last kind of luck is the weirdest, hardest kind, where you build a unique character, a unique brand, a unique mindset, which causes luck to find you.

For example, let's say you're the best person in the world at deep-sea diving. You're known to take on deep-sea dives nobody else will even dare to attempt. By sheer luck, somebody finds a sunken treasure ship off the coast they can't get to. Well, their luck just became your luck, because they're going to come to you to get to the treasure, and you're going to get paid for it.

This is an extreme example, but it shows how one person had blind luck finding the treasure. Them coming to you to extract it and give you half is not blind luck. You created your own luck. You put yourself in a position to capitalize on luck or to attract luck when nobody else created the opportunity for themselves. To get rich without getting lucky, we want to be deterministic. We don't want to leave it to chance.

> Ways to get lucky:
>
> - Hope luck finds you.
> - Hustle until you stumble into it.
> - Prepare the mind and be sensitive to chances others miss.
> - Become the best at what you do. Refine what you do until this is true. Opportunity will seek you out. Luck becomes your destiny.

It starts becoming so deterministic, it stops being luck. The definition starts fading from luck to destiny. To summarize the fourth type: build your character in a certain way, then your character becomes your destiny.

One of the things I think is important to make money is having a reputation that makes people do deals through you. Remember the example of being a great diver where treasure hunters will come and give you a piece of the treasure for your diving skills.

If you are a trusted, reliable, high-integrity, long-term-thinking dealmaker, when other people want to do deals but don't know how to do them in a trustworthy manner with strangers, they will literally approach you and give you a cut of the deal just because of the integrity and reputation you've built up.

Warren Buffett gets offered deals to buy companies, buy warrants, bail out banks, and do things other people can't do because of his reputation. Of course, he has accountability on the line, and he has a strong brand on the line.

Your character and your reputation are things you can build, which will let you take advantage of opportunities other people may characterize as lucky, but you know it wasn't luck. My co-founder Nivi said, "In a long-term game, it seems that everybody is making each other rich. And in a short-term game, it seems like everybody is making themselves rich."

I think that is a brilliant formulation. In a long-term game, it's positive sum. We're all baking the pie together. We're trying to make it as big as possible. And in a short-term game, we're cutting up the pie.

How important is networking?

I think business networking is a complete waste of time. And I know there are people and companies popularizing this concept because it serves them and their business model well, but the reality is if you're building something interesting, you will always have more people who will want to know you. Trying to build business relationships well in advance of doing business is a complete waste of time. I have a much more comfortable philosophy: "Be a maker who makes something interesting people want. Show your craft, practice your craft, and the right people will eventually find you."

And once you've met someone, how do you determine if you can trust someone? What signals do you pay attention to?

If someone is talking a lot about how honest they are, they're probably dishonest. That is just a little telltale indicator I've learned. When someone spends too much time talking about their own values or they're talking themselves up, they're covering for something.

> Sharks eat well but live a life surrounded by sharks.

I have great people in my life who are extremely successful, very desirable (like everybody wants to be their friend), very smart. Yet, I've seen them do one or two things slightly not great to other people. The first time, I'll say, "Hey, I don't think you should do this to that other person. Not because you won't get away with it. You will get away with it, but because it will hurt you in the end."

Not in some cosmic, karma kind of way, but I believe deep down we all know who we are. You cannot hide anything from yourself. Your own failures are written within your psyche, and they are obvious to you. If you have too many of these moral shortcomings, you will not respect yourself. The worst outcome in this world is not having self-esteem. If you don't love yourself, who will?

I think you just have to be very careful about doing things you are fundamentally not going to be proud of, because they will damage you. The first time someone acts this way, I will warn them. By the way, nobody changes. Then I just distance myself from them. I cut them out of my life. I just have this saying inside my head: "The closer you want to get to me, the better your values have to be."

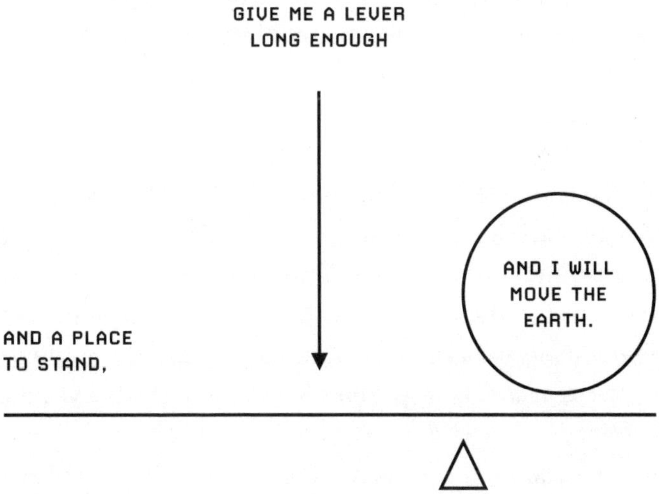

BE PATIENT

One thing I figured out later in life is generally (at least in the tech business in Silicon Valley), great people have great outcomes. You just have to be patient. Every person I met at the beginning of my career twenty years ago, where I looked at them and said, "Wow, that guy or gal is super capable—so smart and dedicated"...all of them, almost without exception, became extremely successful. You just had to give them a long enough timescale. It never happens in the timescale you want, or they want, but it does happen.

> Apply specific knowledge with leverage and eventually, you will get what you deserve.

It takes time—even once you have all of these pieces in place, there is an indeterminate amount of time you have to put in. If you're counting, you'll run out of patience before success actually arrives.

Everybody wants to get rich immediately, but the world is an efficient place; immediate doesn't work. You do have to put in the time. You do have to put in the hours, and so I think you have to put yourself in the position with the specific knowledge, with accountability, with leverage, with the authentic skill set you have, to be the best in the world at what you do.

You have to enjoy it and keep doing it, keep doing it, and keep doing it. Don't keep track, and don't keep count because if you do, you will run out of time.

The most common bad advice I hear is: "You're too young." Most of history was built by young people. They just got credit when they were older. The only way to truly learn something is by doing it. Yes, listen to guidance. But don't wait.

> People are oddly consistent. Karma is just you, repeating your patterns, virtues, and flaws until you finally get what you deserve.
>
> Always pay it forward. And don't keep count.

This is not to say it's easy. It's not easy. It's actually really freaking hard. It is the hardest thing you will do. But it's also rewarding. Look at the kids who are born rich—they have no meaning to their lives.

Your real résumé is just a catalog of all your suffering. If I ask you to describe your real life to yourself, and you look back from your deathbed at the interesting things you've done, it's all going to be around the sacrifices you made, the hard things you did.

However, anything you're given doesn't matter. You have your four limbs, your brain, your head, your skin—that's all for granted. You have to do hard things anyway to create your own meaning in life. Making money is a fine thing to choose. Go struggle. It is hard. I'm not going to say it's easy. It's really hard, but the tools are all available. It's all out there.

Money buys you freedom in the material world. It's not going to make you happy, it's not going to solve your health problems, it's not going to make your family great, it's not going to make you fit, it's not going to make you calm. But it will solve a lot of external problems. It's a reasonable step to go ahead and make money.

What making money will do is solve your money problems. It will remove a set of things that could get in the way of being happy, but it is not going to make you happy. I know many very wealthy people who are unhappy. Most of the time, the person you have to become to make money is a high-anxiety, high-stress, hard-working, competitive person. When you have done that for twenty, thirty, forty, fifty years, and you suddenly make money, you can't turn it off. You've trained yourself to be a high-anxiety person. Then, you have to learn how to be happy.

Let's get you rich first. I'm very practical about it because, you know, Buddha was a prince. He started off really rich, then he got to go off in the woods.

In the old days, if you wanted to be peaceful inside, you would become a monk. You would give up everything, renounce sex, children, money, politics, science, technology, everything, and you would go out in the woods by yourself. You had to give everything up to be free inside.

Today, with this wonderful invention called money, you can store it in a bank account. You can work really hard, do great things for society, and society will give you money for things it wants but doesn't know how to get. You can save money, you can live a little below your means, and you can find a certain freedom.

That will give you the time and the energy to pursue your own internal peace and happiness. I believe the solution to making everybody happy is to give them what they want.

Let's get them all rich.

Let's get them all fit and healthy.

Then, let's get them all happy.

> Amazing how many people confuse wealth and wisdom.

I BUILDING JUDGMENT

There's no shortcut to smart.

JUDGMENT

If you want to make the maximum amount of money possible, if you want to get rich over your life in a deterministically predictable way, stay on the bleeding edge of trends and study technology, design, and art—become really good at something.

> You don't get rich by spending your time to save money.
>
> You get rich by saving your time to make money.

Hard work is really overrated. How hard you work matters a lot less in the modern economy.

What is underrated?

Judgment. Judgment is underrated.

Can you define judgment?

My definition of wisdom is knowing the long-term consequences of your actions. Wisdom applied to external problems is judgment. They're highly linked; knowing the long-term consequences of your actions and then making the right decision to capitalize on that.

> In an age of leverage, one correct decision can win everything.

> Without hard work, you'll develop neither judgment nor leverage.

You have to put in the time, but the judgment is more important. The direction you're heading in matters more than how fast you move, especially with leverage. Picking the direction you're heading in for every decision is far, far more important than how much force you apply. Just pick the right direction to start walking in, and start walking.

HOW TO THINK CLEARLY

> "Clear thinker" is a better compliment than "smart."

Real knowledge is intrinsic, and it's built from the ground up. To use a math example, you can't understand trigonometry without understanding arithmetic and geometry. Basically, if someone is using a lot of fancy words and a lot of big concepts, they probably don't know what they're talking about. I think the smartest people can explain things to a child. If you can't explain it to a child, then you don't know it. It's a common saying and it's very true.

Richard Feynman very famously does this in "Six Easy Pieces," one of his early physics lectures. He basically explains mathematics in three pages. He starts from the number line—counting—and then he goes all the way up to precalculus. He just builds it up through an unbroken chain of logic. He doesn't rely on any definitions.

The really smart thinkers are clear thinkers. They understand the basics at a very, very fundamental level. I would rather understand the basics really well than memorize all kinds of complicated concepts I can't stitch together and can't rederive from the basics. If you can't rederive concepts from the basics as you need them, you're lost. You're just memorizing.

The advanced concepts in a field are less proven. We use them to signal insider knowledge, but we'd be better off nailing the basics.

> Clear thinkers appeal to their own authority.

Part of making effective decisions boils down to dealing with reality. How do you make sure you're dealing with reality when you're making decisions?

By not having a strong sense of self or judgments or mind presence. The "monkey mind" will always respond with this regurgitated emotional response to what it thinks the world should be. Those desires will cloud your reality. This happens a lot of times when people are mixing politics and business.

The number one thing clouding us from being able to see reality is we have preconceived notions of the way it should be.

One definition of a moment of suffering is "the moment when you see things exactly the way they are." This whole time, you've been convinced your business is doing great, and really, you've ignored the signs it's not doing well. Then, your business fails, and you suffer because you've been putting off reality. You've been hiding it from yourself.

The good news is, the moment of suffering—when you're in pain—is a moment of truth. It is a moment where you're forced to embrace reality the way it actually is. Then, you can make meaningful change and progress. You can only make progress when you're starting with the truth.

The hard thing is seeing the truth. To see the truth, you have to get your ego out of the way because your ego doesn't want to face the truth. The smaller you can make your ego, the less conditioned you can make your reactions, the less desires you can have about the outcome you want, the easier it will be to see the reality.

> What we wish to be true clouds our perception of what is true. Suffering is the moment when we can no longer deny reality.

Imagine we're going through something difficult like a breakup, a job loss, a business failure, or a health problem, and our friends are advising us. When we're advising them, the answer is obvious. It comes to us in a minute, and we tell them exactly, "Oh that girl, get over her, she wasn't good for you anyway. You'll be happier. Trust me. You'll find someone."

You know the correct answer, but your friend can't see it, because they're in the moment of suffering and pain. They're still wishing reality was different. The problem isn't reality. The problem is their desire is colliding with reality and preventing them from seeing the truth, no matter how much you say it. The same thing happens when I make decisions.

The more desire I have for something to work out a certain way, the less likely I am to see the truth. Especially in business, if something isn't going well, I try to acknowledge it publicly and I try to acknowledge it publicly in front of my co-founders and friends and co-workers. Then, I'm not hiding it from anybody else. If I'm not hiding it from anybody, I'm not going to delude myself from what's actually going on.

> What you feel tells you nothing about the facts—it merely tells you something about your estimate of the facts.

It's actually really important to have empty space. If you don't have a day or two every week in your calendar where you're not always in meetings, and you're not always busy, then you're not going to be able to think.

You're not going to be able to have good ideas for your business. You're not going to be able to make good judgments. I also encourage taking at least one day a week (preferably two, because if you budget two, you'll end up with one) where you just have time to think.

It's only after you're bored you have the great ideas. It's never going to be when you're stressed, or busy, running around or rushed. Make the time.

> Very smart people tend to be weird since they insist on thinking everything through for themselves.

A contrarian isn't one who always objects—that's a conformist of a different sort. A contrarian reasons independently from the ground up and resists pressure to conform.

Cynicism is easy. Mimicry is easy.
Optimistic contrarians are the rarest breed.

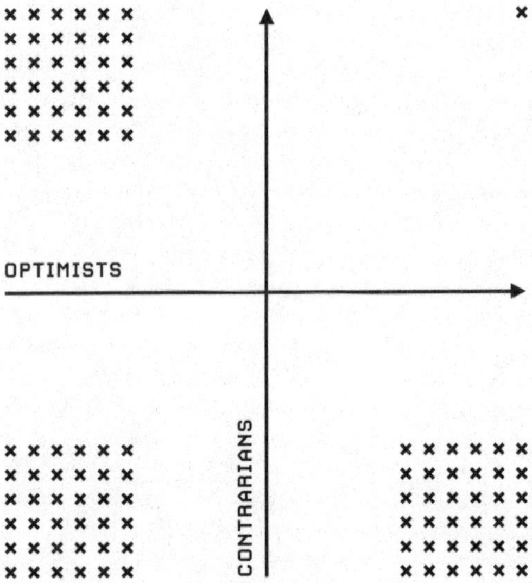

SHED YOUR IDENTITY TO SEE REALITY

Our egos are constructed in our formative years—our first two decades. They get constructed by our environment, our parents, society. Then, we spend the rest of our life trying to make our ego happy. We interpret anything new through our ego: "How do I change the external world to make it more how I would like it to be?"

> "Tension is who you think you should be.
> Relaxation is who you are."
>
> —Buddhist saying

You absolutely need habits to function. You cannot solve every problem in life as if it is the first time it's thrown at you. We accumulate all these habits. We put them in the bundle of identity, ego, ourselves, and then we get attached to them. "I'm Naval. This is the way I am."

It's really important to be able to uncondition yourself, to be able to take your habits apart and say, "Okay, this is a habit I probably picked up when I was a toddler trying to get my parent's attention. Now I've reinforced it and reinforced it, and I call it a part of my identity. Does it still serve me? Does it make me happier? Does it make me healthier? Does it make me accomplish whatever I set out to accomplish?"

I'm less habitual than most people. I don't like to structure my day. To the extent I have habits, I try to make them more deliberate rather than accidents of history.

> Any belief you took in a package (ex. Democrat, Catholic, American) is suspect and should be re-evaluated from base principles.

I try not to have too much I've pre-decided. I think creating identities and labels locks you in and keeps you from seeing the truth.

> To be honest, speak without identity.

I used to identify as libertarian, but then I would find myself defending positions I hadn't really thought through because they're a part of the libertarian canon. If all your beliefs line up into neat little bundles, you should be highly suspicious.

I don't like to self-identify on almost any level anymore, which keeps me from having too many of these so-called stable beliefs.

> We each have a contrarian belief society rejects. But the more our own identity and local tribe reject it, the more real it likely is.

There are two attractive lessons about suffering in the long term. It can make you accept the world the way it is. The other lesson is it can make your ego change in an extremely hard way.

Maybe you're a competitive athlete, and you get injured badly, like Bruce Lee. You have to accept being an athlete is not your entire identity, and maybe you can forge a new identity as a philosopher.

> Facebook redesigns. Twitter redesigns. Personalities, careers, and teams also need redesigns. There are no permanent solutions in a dynamic system.

TENSION IS WHO YOU THINK YOU SHOULD BE.

RELAXATION IS WHO YOU ARE.

LEARN THE SKILLS OF DECISION-MAKING

The classical virtues are all decision-making heuristics to make one optimize for the long term rather than for the short term.

> Self-serving conclusions should have a higher bar.

I do view a lot of my goals over the next few years of unconditioning previous learned responses or habituated responses, so I can make decisions more cleanly in the moment without relying on memory or prepackaged heuristics and judgments.

> Almost all biases are time-saving heuristics. For important decisions, discard memory and identity, and focus on the problem.

Radical honesty just means I want to be free. Part of being free means I can say what I think and think what I say. They're highly congruent and integrated. Theoretical physicist Richard Feynman famously said, "You should never, ever fool anybody, and you are the easiest person to fool." The moment you tell somebody something dishonest, you've lied to yourself. Then you'll start believing your own lie, which will disconnect you from reality and take you down the wrong road.

> I never ask if "I like it" or "I don't like it." I think "this is what it is" or "this is what it isn't."
>
> —Richard Feynman

It's really important for me to be honest. I don't go out of my way volunteering negative or nasty things. I would combine radical honesty with an old rule Warren Buffett has, which is praise specifically, criticize generally. I try to follow this. I don't always follow it, but I think I follow it enough to have made a difference in my life.

If you have a criticism of someone, then don't criticize the person—criticize the general approach or criticize the class of activities. If you have to praise somebody, then always try and find the person who is the best example of what you're praising and praise the person, specifically. Then people's egos and identities, which we all have, don't work against you. They work for you.

Any advice on developing capacity for instinctual blunt honesty?

Tell everyone. Start now. It doesn't have to be blunt. Charisma is the ability to project confidence and love at the same time. It's almost always possible to be honest and positive.

As an investor and CEO of AngelList, you're paid to be right when other people are wrong. Do you have a process around how you make decisions?

Yes. Decision-making is everything. In fact, someone who makes decisions right 80 percent of the time instead of 70 percent of the time will be valued and compensated in the market hundreds of times more.

I think people have a hard time understanding a fundamental fact of leverage. If I manage $1 billion and I'm right 10 percent more often than somebody else, my decision-making creates $100 million worth of value on a judgment call. With modern technology and large workforces and capital, our decisions are leveraged more and more.

If you can be more right and more rational, you're going to get nonlinear returns in your life. I love the blog *Farnam Street* because it really focuses on helping you be more accurate, an overall better decision-maker. Decision-making is everything.

> The more you know, the less you diversify.

COLLECT MENTAL MODELS

During decision-making, the brain is a memory prediction machine.

A lousy way to do memory prediction is "X happened in the past, therefore X will happen in the future." It's too based on specific circumstances. What you want is principles. You want mental models.

The best mental models I have found came through evolution, game theory, and Charlie Munger. Charlie Munger is Warren Buffett's partner. Very good investor. He has tons and tons of great mental models. Author and trader Nassim Taleb has great mental models. Benjamin Franklin had great mental models. I basically load my head full of mental models.

I use my tweets and other people's tweets as maxims that help compress my own learnings and recall them. The brain space is finite—you have finite neurons—so you can almost think of these as pointers, addresses, or mnemonics to help you remember deep-seated principles where you have the underlying experience to back it up.

If you don't have the underlying experience, then it just reads like a collection of quotes. It's cool, it's inspirational for a moment, maybe you'll make a nice poster out of it. But then you forget it and move on. Mental models are really just compact ways for you to recall your own knowledge.

EVOLUTION

I think a lot of modern society can be explained through evolution. One theory is civilization exists to answer the question of who gets to mate. If you look around, from a purely sexual selection perspective, sperm is abundant and eggs are scarce. It's an allocation problem.

Literally all of the works of mankind and womankind can be traced down to people trying to solve this problem.

Evolution, thermodynamics, information theory, and complexity have explanatory and predictive power in many aspects of life.

INVERSION

I don't believe I have the ability to say what is going to work. Rather, I try to eliminate what's not going to work. I think being successful is just about not making mistakes. It's not about having correct judgment. It's about avoiding incorrect judgments.

COMPLEXITY THEORY

I was really into complexity theory back in the mid-90s. The more I got into it, the more I understand the limits of our knowledge and the limits of our prediction capability. Complexity has been super helpful to me. It has helped me come to a system that operates in the face of ignorance. I believe we are fundamentally ignorant and very, very bad at predicting the future.

ECONOMICS

Microeconomics and game theory are fundamental. I don't think you can be successful in business or even navigate most of our modern capitalist society without an extremely good understanding of supply-and-demand, labor-versus-capital, game theory, and those kinds of things.

> Ignore the noise. The market will decide.

PRINCIPAL-AGENT PROBLEM

To me, the principal-agent problem is the single most fundamental problem in microeconomics. If you do not understand the principal-agent problem, you will not know how to navigate your way through the world. It is important if you want to build a successful company or be successful in your dealings.

It's a very simple concept. Julius Caesar famously said, "If you want it done, then go. And if not, then send." What he meant was, if you want it done right, then you have to go yourself and do it. When you are the principal, then you are the owner—you care, and you will do a great job. When you are the agent and you are doing it on somebody else's behalf, you can do a bad job. You just don't care. You optimize for yourself rather than for the principal's assets.

The smaller the company, the more everyone feels like a principal. The less you feel like an agent, the better the job you're going to do. The more closely you can tie someone's compensation to the exact value they're creating, the more you turn them into a principal, and the less you turn them into an agent.

I think at a core fundamental level, we understand this. We're attracted to principals, and we all bond with principals, but the media and modern society spend a lot of time brainwashing you about needing an agent, an agent being important, and the agent being knowledgeable.

COMPOUND INTEREST

Compound interest—most of you should know it in the finance context. If you don't, crack open a microeconomics textbook. It's worth reading a microeconomics textbook from start to finish.

An example of compound interest—let's say you're earning 10 percent a year on your $1. The first year, you make 10 percent, and you end up with $1.10. The next year, you end up with $1.21, and the next year $1.33. It keeps adding onto itself. If you're compounding at 30 percent per year for thirty years, you don't just end up with ten or twenty times your money—you end up with thousands of times your money.

In the intellectual domain, compound interest rules. When

you look at a business with one hundred users growing at a compound rate of 20 percent per month, it can very, very quickly stack up to having millions of users. Sometimes, even the founders of these companies are surprised by how large the business scales.

BASIC MATH

I think basic mathematics is really underrated. If you're going to make money, if you're going to invest money, your basic math should be really good. You don't need to learn geometry, trigonometry, calculus, or any of the complicated stuff if you're just going into business. But you want arithmetic, probability, and statistics. Those are extremely important. Crack open a basic math book, and make sure you are really good at multiplying, dividing, compounding, probability, and statistics.

BLACK SWANS

There's a new branch of probability statistics, which is really around tail events. Black swans are extreme probabilities. Again, I have to refer back to Nassim Taleb, who I think is one of the greatest philosopher-scientists of our times. He's really done a lot of pioneering work on this.

CALCULUS

Calculus is useful to know, to understand the rates of change and how nature works. But it's more important to understand the principles of calculus—where you're measuring the change in small discrete or small continuous events. It's not important you solve integrals or do derivations on demand, because you're not going to need to in the business world.

FALSIFIABILITY

Least understood, but the most important principle for anyone claiming "science" on their side—falsifiability. If it doesn't make falsifiable predictions, it's not science. For you to believe something is true, it should have predictive power, and it must be falsifiable.

I think macroeconomics, because it doesn't make falsifiable predictions (which is the hallmark of science), has become corrupted. You never have a counterexample when studying the economy. You can never take the US economy and run two different experiments at the same time.

IF YOU CAN'T DECIDE, THE ANSWER IS NO.

If I'm faced with a difficult choice, such as:

→ Should I marry this person?
→ Should I take this job?
→ Should I buy this house?
→ Should I move to this city?
→ Should I go into business with this person?

If you cannot decide, the answer is no. And the reason is, modern society is full of options. There are tons and tons of options. We live on a planet of seven billion people, and we are connected to everybody on the internet. There are hundreds of thousands of careers available to you. There are so many choices.

You're biologically not built to realize how many choices there are. Historically, we've all evolved in tribes of 150 people. When someone comes along, they may be your only option for a partner.

When you choose something, you get locked in for a long time. Starting a business may take ten years. You start a relationship that will be five years or maybe more. You move to a city for ten to twenty years. These are very, very long-lived decisions. It's very, very important we only say yes when we are pretty certain. You're never going to be absolutely certain, but you're going to be very certain.

If you find yourself creating a spreadsheet for a decision with a list of yes's and no's, pros and cons, checks and balances, why this is good or bad...forget it. If you cannot decide, the answer is no.

RUN UPHILL

> Simple heuristic: If you're evenly split on a difficult decision, take the path more painful in the short term.

If you have two choices to make, and they're relatively equal choices, take the path more difficult and more painful in the short term.

What's actually going on is one of these paths requires short-term pain. And the other path leads to pain further out in the future. And what your brain is doing through conflict-avoidance is trying to push off the short-term pain.

By definition, if the two are even and one has short-term pain, that path has long-term gain associated. With the law of compound interest, long-term gain is what you want to go toward.

Your brain is overvaluing the side with the short-term happiness and trying to avoid the one with short-term pain.

So you have to cancel the tendency out (it's a powerful subconscious tendency) by leaning into the pain. As you know, most of the gains in life come from suffering in the short term so you can get paid in the long term.

Working out for me is not fun; I suffer in the short term, I feel pain. But then in the long term, I'm better off because I have muscles or I'm healthier.

If I am reading a book and I'm getting confused, it is just like working out and the muscle getting sore or tired, except now my brain is being overwhelmed. In the long run I'm getting smarter because I'm absorbing new concepts from working at the limit or edge of my capability.

So you generally want to lean into things with short-term pain, but long-term gain.

What are the most efficient ways to build new mental models?

Read a lot—just read.

> Reading science, math, and philosophy one hour per day will likely put you at the upper echelon of human success within seven years.

LEARN TO LOVE TO READ

(Specific recommendations for books, blogs, and more are in "Naval's Recommended Reading" section.)

The genuine love for reading itself, when cultivated, is a superpower. We live in the age of Alexandria, when every book and every piece of knowledge ever written down is a fingertip away. The means of learning are abundant—it's the desire to learn that is scarce.

> Reading was my first love.

I remember my grandparents' house in India. I'd be a little kid on the floor going through all of my grandfather's *Reader's Digests*, which is all he had to read. Now, of course, there's a smorgasbord of information out there—anybody can read anything all the time. Back then, it was much more limited. I would read comic books, storybooks, whatever I could get my hands on.

I think I always loved to read because I'm actually an antisocial introvert. I was lost in the world of words and ideas from an early age. I think some of it comes from the happy circumstance that when I was young, nobody forced me to read certain things.

I think there's a tendency among parents and teachers to say, "Oh, you should read this, but don't read that." I read a lot which (by today's standards) would be considered mental junk food.

> Read what you love until you love to read.

You almost have to read the stuff you're reading, because you're into it. You don't need any other reason. There's no mission here to accomplish. Just read because you enjoy it.

These days, I find myself rereading as much (or more) as I do reading. A tweet from @illacertus said, "I don't want to read everything. I just want to read the 100 great books over and over again." I think there's a lot to that idea. It's really more about identifying the great books for you because different books speak to different people. Then, you can really absorb those.

> Reading a book isn't a race—the better the book, the more slowly it should be absorbed.

I don't know about you, but I have very poor attention. I skim. I speed read. I jump around. I could not tell you specific passages or quotes from books. At some deep level, you absorb them, and they become threads in the tapestry of your psyche. They kind of weave in there.

I'm sure you've had this feeling where you pick up a book and start reading it, and you're like, "This is pretty interesting. This is pretty good." You're getting this increasing sense of deja vu. Then halfway through the book, you realize, "I've read this book before." That's perfectly fine. It means you were ready to reread it.

> I don't actually read a lot of books. I pick up a lot of books and only get through a few which form the foundation of my knowledge.

The reality is, I don't actually read much compared to what people think. I probably read one to two hours a day. That puts me in the top .00001 percent. I think that alone accounts for any material success I've had in my life and any intelligence I might have. Real people don't read an hour a day. Real people, I think, read a minute a day or less. Making it an actual habit is the most important thing.

It almost doesn't matter what you read. Eventually, you will read enough things (and your interests will lead you there) that it will dramatically improve your life. Just like the best workout for you is one you're excited enough to do every day, I would say for books, blogs, tweets, or whatever—anything with ideas and information and learning—the best ones to read are the ones you're excited about reading all the time.

> "As long as I have a book in my hand, I don't feel like I'm wasting time."
>
> —Charlie Munger

Everyone's brain works differently. Some people love to take notes. Actually, my notetaking is Twitter. I read and read and read. If I have some fundamental "ah-ha" insight or concept, Twitter forces me to distill it into a few characters. Then I try and put it out there as an aphorism. Then I get attacked by random people who point out all kinds of obvious exceptions and jump down my throat. Then I think, "Why did I do this again?"

> Pointing out obvious exceptions implies either the target isn't smart or you aren't.

When you first pick up a book, are you skimming for something interesting? How do you go about reading it? Do you just flip to a random page and start reading? What's your process?

I'll start at the beginning, but I'll move fast. If it's not interesting, I'll just start flipping ahead, skimming, or speed reading. If it doesn't grab my attention within the first chapter in a meaningful, positive way, I'll either drop the book or skip ahead a few chapters.

I don't believe in delayed gratification when there are an infinite number of books out there to read. There are so many great books.

> The number of books completed is a vanity metric. As you know more, you leave more books unfinished. Focus on new concepts with predictive power.

Generally, I'll skim. I'll fast forward. I'll try and find a part to catch my attention. Most books have one point to make. (Obviously, this is nonfiction. I'm not talking about fiction.) They have one point to make, they make it, and then they give you example after example after example after example, and they apply it to explain everything in the world. Once I feel like I've gotten the gist, I feel very comfortable putting the book down. There's a lot of these, what I would call pseudoscience bestsellers...People are like, "Oh, did you read this book?" I always say yes, but the reality is I read maybe two chapters of it. I got the gist.

> If they wrote it to make money, don't read it.

What practices do you follow to internalize/organize information from reading books?

Explain what you learned to someone else. Teaching forces learning.

> It's not about "educated" vs. "uneducated." It's about "likes to read" and "doesn't like to read."

What can I do for the next sixty days to become a clearer, more independent thinker?

Read the greats in math, science, and philosophy. Ignore your contemporaries and news. Avoid tribal identification. Put truth above social approval.

> Study logic and math, because once you've mastered them, you won't fear any book.

No book in the library should scare you. Whether it's a math, physics, electrical engineering, sociology, or economics book. You should be able to take any book down off the shelf and read it. A number of them are going to be too difficult for you. That's okay—read them anyway. Then go back and reread them and reread them.

When you're reading a book and you're confused, that confusion is similar to the pain you get in the gym when you're working out. But you're building mental muscles instead of physical muscles. Learn how to learn and read the books.

The problem with saying "just read" is there is so much junk out there. There are as many different kinds of authors as there are people. Many of them are going to write lots of junk.

I have people in my life I consider to be very well-read who aren't very smart. The reason is because even though they're very well-read, they read the wrong things in the wrong order. They started out reading a set of false or just weakly true things, and those formed the axioms of the foundation for their worldview. Then, when new things come, they judge the new idea based on a foundation they already built. Your foundation is critical.

> Because most people are intimidated by math and can't independently critique it, they overvalue opinions backed with math/pseudoscience.

When it comes to reading, make sure your foundation is very, very high quality.

The best way to have a high-quality foundation (you may not love this answer), but the trick is to stick to science and to stick to the basics. Generally, there are only a few things you can read people don't disagree with. Very few people disagree 2+2=4, right? That is serious knowledge. Mathematics is a solid foundation.

Similarly, the hard sciences are a solid foundation. Microeconomics is a solid foundation. The moment you start wandering outside of these solid foundations you're in trouble because now you don't know what's true and what's false. I would focus as much as I could on having solid foundations.

It's better to be really great at arithmetic and geometry than to be deep into advanced mathematics. I would read microeconomics all day long—Microeconomics 101.

Another way to do this is to read originals and read classics. If you're interested in evolution, read Charles Darwin. Don't begin with Richard Dawkins (even though I think he's great). Read him later; read Darwin first.

If you want to learn macroeconomics, first read Adam Smith, read von Mises, or read Hayek. Start with the original philosophers of the economy. If you're into communist or socialist ideas (which I'm personally not), start by reading Karl Marx. Don't read the current interpretation someone is feeding you about how things should be done and run.

If you start with the originals as your foundations, then you have enough of a worldview and understanding that you won't fear any book. Then you can just learn. If you're a perpetual learning machine, you will never be out of options for how to make money. You can always see what's coming up in society, what the value is, where the demand is, and you can learn to come up to speed.

> To think clearly, understand the basics. If you're memorizing advanced concepts without being able to re-derive them as needed, you're lost.

We're now in a day and age of Twitter and Facebook. We're getting bite-sized, pithy wisdom, which is really hard to absorb. Books are very difficult to read as a modern person because we've been trained. We have two contradictory pieces of training:

One is our attention span has gone through the floor because we're hit with so much information all the time. We want to skip, summarize, and cut to the chase.

> Twitter has made me a worse reader but a much better writer.

On the other hand, we're also taught from a young age to finish your books. Books are sacred—when you go to school and you're assigned to read a book, you have to finish the book. Over time, we forget how to read books. Everyone I know is stuck on some book.

I'm sure you're stuck on something right now—it's page 332,

you can't go any further, but you know you should finish the book. So what do you do? You give up reading books for a while.

For me, giving up reading was a tragedy. I grew up on books, then I switched to blogs, then I switched to Twitter and Facebook, and I realized I wasn't actually learning anything. I was just taking little dopamine snacks all day long. I was getting my little 140-character burst of dopamine. I would Tweet, then look to see who retweeted my Tweet. It's a fun and wonderful thing, but it's a game I was playing.

I realized I had to go back to reading books.

I knew it was a very hard problem because my brain had now been trained to spend time on Facebook, Twitter, and these other bite-sized pieces.

I came up with this hack where I started treating books as throwaway blog posts or bite-sized tweets or posts. I felt no obligation to finish any book. Now, when someone mentions a book to me, I buy it. At any given time, I'm reading somewhere between ten and twenty books. I'm flipping through them.

If the book is getting a little boring, I'll skip ahead. Sometimes, I start reading a book in the middle because some paragraph caught my eye. I'll just continue from there, and I feel no obligation whatsoever to finish the book. All of a sudden, books are back into my reading library. That's great, because there is ancient wisdom in books.

When solving problems: the older the problem, the older the solution.

If you're trying to learn how to drive a car or fly a plane, you should read something written in the modern age because this problem was created in the modern age and the solution is great in the modern age.

If you're talking about an old problem like how to keep your body healthy, how to stay calm and peaceful, what kinds of value systems are good, how you raise a family, and those kinds of things, the older solutions are probably better.

Any book that survived for two thousand years has been filtered through many people. The general principles are more likely to be correct. I wanted to get back into reading these sorts of books.

> You know that song you can't get out of your head? All thoughts work that way. Careful what you read.

A calm mind, a fit body, and a house full of love.

These things cannot be bought.

They must be earned.

PART II

HAPPINESS

> The three big ones in life are wealth, health, and happiness. We pursue them in that order, but their importance is reverse.

I LEARNING HAPPINESS

> Don't take yourself so seriously. You're just a monkey with a plan.

HAPPINESS IS LEARNED

Ten years ago, if you would have asked me how happy I was, I would have dismissed the question. I didn't want to talk about it.

On a scale of 1–10, I would have said 2/10 or 3/10. Maybe 4/10 on my best days. But I did not value being happy.

Today, I am a 9/10. And yes, having money helps, but it's actually a very small piece of it. Most of it comes from learning over the years my own happiness is the most important thing to me, and I've cultivated it with a lot of techniques.

> Maybe happiness is not something you inherit or even choose, but a highly personal skill that can be learned, like fitness or nutrition.

Happiness is a very evolving thing, I think, like all the great questions. When you're a little kid, you go to your mom and ask, "What happens when we die? Is there a Santa Claus? Is there a God? Should I be happy? Who should I marry?" Those kinds of things. There are no glib answers because no answers apply to everybody. These kinds of questions ultimately do have answers, but they have personal answers.

The answer that works for me is going to be nonsense to you, and vice versa. Whatever happiness means to me, it means something different to you. I think it's very important to explore what these definitions are.

For some people I know, it's a flow state. For some people, it's satisfaction. For some people, it's a feeling of contentment. My definition keeps evolving. The answer I would have given you a year ago will be different than what I tell you now.

Today, I believe happiness is really a default state. Happiness is there when you remove the sense of something missing in your life.

We are highly judgmental survival-and-replication machines. We constantly walk around thinking, "I need this," or "I need that," trapped in the web of desires. Happiness is the state when nothing is missing. When nothing is missing, your mind shuts down and stops running into the past or future to regret something or to plan something.

In that absence, for a moment, you have internal silence. When you have internal silence, then you are content, and you are happy. Feel free to disagree. Again, it's different for everybody.

People mistakenly believe happiness is just about positive thoughts and positive actions. The more I've read, the more I've learned, and the more I've experienced (because I verify this for myself), every positive thought essentially holds within it a negative thought. It is a contrast to something negative. The *Tao Te Ching* says this more articulately than I ever could, but it's all duality and polarity. If I say I'm happy, that means I was sad at some point. If I say he's attractive, then somebody else is unattractive. Every positive thought even has a seed of a negative thought within it and vice versa, which is why a lot of greatness in life comes out of suffering. You have to view the negative before you can aspire to and appreciate the positive.

To me, happiness is not about positive thoughts. It's not about negative thoughts. It's about the absence of desire, especially the absence of desire for external things. The fewer desires I can have, the more I can accept the current state of things, the less my mind is moving, because the mind really exists in motion toward the future or the past. The more present I am, the happier and more content I will be. If I latch onto a feeling, if I say, "Oh, I'm happy now," and I want to stay happy, then I'm going to drop out of that happiness. Now, suddenly, the mind is moving. It's trying to attach to something. It's trying to create a permanent situation out of a temporary situation.

Happiness to me is mainly not suffering, not desiring, not thinking too much about the future or the past, really embracing the present moment and the reality of what is, and the way it is.

> If you ever want to have peace in your life, you have to move beyond good and evil.

Nature has no concept of happiness or unhappiness. Nature follows unbroken mathematical laws and a chain of cause and effect from the Big Bang to now. Everything is perfect exactly the way it is. It is only in our particular minds we are unhappy or not happy, and things are perfect or imperfect because of what we desire.

The world just reflects your own feelings back at you. Reality is neutral. Reality has no judgments. To a tree, there is no concept of right or wrong, good or bad. You're born, you have a whole set of sensory experiences and stimulations (lights, colors, and sounds), and then you die. How you choose to interpret them is up to you—you have that choice.

This is what I mean when I say happiness is a choice. If you believe it's a choice, you can start working on it.

> There are no external forces affecting your emotions—as much as it may feel that way.

I've also come to believe in the complete and utter insignificance of the self, and I think that helps a lot. For example, if you thought you were the most important thing in the Universe, then you would have to bend the entire Universe to your will. If you're the most important thing in the Universe, then how could it not conform to your desires. If it doesn't conform to your desires, something is wrong.

However, if you view yourself as a bacteria or an amoeba—or if you view all of your works as writing on water or building castles in the sand, then you have no expectation for how life should "actually" be. Life is just the way it is. When you accept that, you have no cause to be happy or unhappy. Those things almost don't apply.

> Happiness is what's there when you remove the sense that something is missing in your life.

What you're left with in that neutral state is not neutrality. I think people believe neutrality would be a very bland existence. No, this is the existence little children live. If you look at little children, on balance, they're generally pretty happy because they are really immersed in the environment and the moment, without any thought of how it should be given their personal preferences and desires. I think the neutral state is actually a perfection state. One can be very happy as long as one isn't too caught up in their own head.

Our lives are a blink of a firefly in the night. You're just barely here. You have to make the most of every minute, which doesn't mean you chase some stupid desire for your entire life. What it means is every second you have on this planet is very precious, and it's your responsibility to make sure you're happy and interpreting everything in the best possible way.

> We think of ourselves as fixed and the world as malleable, but it's really we who are malleable and the world is largely fixed.

Can practicing meditation help you accept reality?

Yeah. But it's amazing how little it helps. [laughs] You can be a long-time meditator, but if someone says the wrong thing in the wrong way, you go back to your ego-driven self. It's almost like you're lifting one-pound weights, but then somebody drops a huge barbell with a stack of plates on your head.

It's absolutely better than doing nothing. But when the actual moment of mental or emotional suffering arrives, it's still never easy. Real happiness only comes as a side-effect of peace. Most of it is going to come from acceptance, not from changing your external environment.

> A rational person can find peace by cultivating indifference to things outside of their control.

I have lowered my identity.

I have lowered the chattering of my mind.

I don't care about things that don't really matter.

I don't get involved in politics.

I don't hang around unhappy people.

I really value my time on this earth.

I read philosophy.

I meditate.

I hang around with happy people.

And it works.

You can very slowly but steadily and methodically improve your happiness baseline, just like you can improve your fitness.

HAPPINESS IS A CHOICE

> Happiness, love, and passion...aren't things you find—they're choices you make.

Happiness is a choice you make and a skill you develop.

The mind is just as malleable as the body. We spend so much time and effort trying to change the external world, other people, and our own bodies—all while accepting ourselves the way we were programmed in our youths.

We accept the voice in our head as the source of all truth. But all of it is malleable, and every day is new. Memory and identity are burdens from the past preventing us from living freely in the present.

HAPPINESS REQUIRES PRESENCE

At any given time, when you're walking down the streets, a very small percentage of your brain is focused on the present. The rest is planning the future or regretting the past. This keeps you from having an incredible experience. It's keeping you from seeing the beauty in everything and for being grateful for where you are. You can literally destroy your happiness if you spend all of your time living in delusions of the future.

> We crave experiences that will make us be present, but the cravings themselves take us from the present moment.

I just don't believe in anything from my past. Anything. No memories. No regrets. No people. No trips. Nothing. A lot of our unhappiness comes from comparing things from the past to the present.

> Anticipation for our vices pulls us into the future. Eliminating vices makes it easier to be present.

There's a great definition I read: "Enlightenment is the space between your thoughts." It means enlightenment isn't something you achieve after thirty years sitting on a mountaintop. It's something you can achieve moment to moment, and you can be enlightened to a certain percent every single day.

> What if this life is the paradise we were promised, and we're just squandering it?

HAPPINESS REQUIRES PEACE

Are happiness and purpose interconnected?

Happiness is such an overloaded word, I'm not even sure what it means. For me these days, happiness is more about peace than it is about joy. I don't think peace and purpose go together.

If it's your internal purpose, the thing you most want to do, then sure, you'll be happy doing it. But an externally inflicted purpose, like "society wants me to do X," "I am the first son of the first son of this, so I should do Y," or "I have this debt or burden I took on," I don't think it will make you happy.

I think a lot of us have this low-level pervasive feeling of anxiety. If you pay attention to your mind, sometimes you're just running around doing your thing and you're not feeling great, and you notice your mind is chattering and chattering about something. Maybe you can't sit still...There's this "nexting" thing where you're sitting in one spot thinking about where you should be next.

It's always the next thing, then the next thing, the next thing after that, then the next thing after that creating this pervasive anxiety.

It's most obvious if you ever just sit down and try and do nothing, nothing. I mean nothing, I mean not read a book, I mean not listen to music, I mean literally just sit down and do nothing. You can't do it, because there's anxiety always trying to make you get up and go, get up and go, get up and go. I think it's important just being aware the anxiety is making you unhappy. The anxiety is just a series of running thoughts.

How I combat anxiety: I don't try and fight it, I just notice I'm anxious because of all these thoughts. I try to figure out, "Would I rather be having this thought right now, or would I rather have my peace?" Because as long as I have my thoughts, I can't have my peace.

You'll notice when I say happiness, I mean peace. When a lot of people say happiness, they mean joy or bliss, but I'll take peace.

> A happy person isn't someone who's happy all the time.
>
> It's someone who effortlessly interprets events in such a way that they don't lose their innate peace.

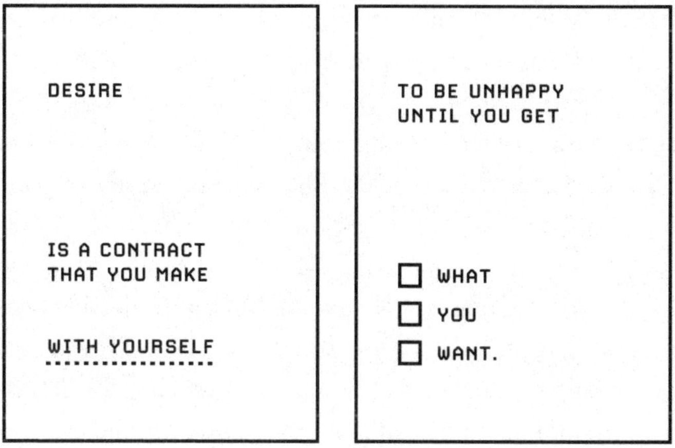

EVERY DESIRE IS A CHOSEN UNHAPPINESS

I think the most common mistake for humanity is believing you're going to be made happy because of some external circumstance. I know that's not original. That's not new. It's fundamental Buddhist wisdom—I'm not taking credit for it. I think I really just recognize it on a fundamental level, including in myself.

We bought a new car. Now, I'm waiting for the new car to arrive. Of course, every night, I'm on the forums reading about the car. Why? It's a silly object. It's a silly car. It's not going to change my life much or at all. I know the instant the car arrives I won't care about it anymore. The thing is, I'm addicted to the desiring. I'm addicted to the idea of this external thing bringing me some kind of happiness and joy, and this is completely delusional.

Looking outside yourself for anything is the fundamental delusion. Not to say you shouldn't do things on the outside. You absolutely should. You're a living creature. There are things you do. You locally reverse entropy. That's why you're here.

You're meant to do something. You're not just meant to lie there in the sand and meditate all day long. You should self-actualize. You should do what you are meant to do.

The idea you're going to change something in the outside world, and that is going to bring you the peace, everlasting joy, and happiness you deserve, is a fundamental delusion we all suffer from, including me. The mistake over and over and over is to say, "Oh, I'll be happy when I get that thing," whatever it is. That is the fundamental mistake we all make, 24/7, all day long.

> The fundamental delusion: There is something out there that will make me happy and fulfilled forever.

Desire is a contract you make with yourself to be unhappy until you get what you want. I don't think most of us realize that's what it is. I think we go about desiring things all day long and then wonder why we're unhappy. I like to stay aware of it, because then I can choose my desires very carefully. I try not to have more than one big desire in my life at any given time, and I also recognize it as the axis of my suffering. I realize the area where I've chosen to be unhappy.

> Desire is a contract you make with yourself to be unhappy until you get what you want.

One thing I've learned recently: it's way more important to perfect your desires than to try to do something you don't 100 percent desire.

When you're young and healthy, you can do more. By doing more, you're actually taking on more and more desires. You don't realize this is slowly destroying your happiness. I find younger people are less happy but more healthy. Older people are more happy but less healthy.

When you're young, you have time. You have health, but you have no money. When you're middle-aged, you have money and you have health, but you have no time. When you're old, you have money and you have time, but you have no health. So the trifecta is trying to get all three at once.

By the time people realize they have enough money, they've lost their time and their health.

SUCCESS DOES NOT EARN HAPPINESS

> Happiness is being satisfied with what you have.
>
> Success comes from dissatisfaction. Choose.

Confucius says you have two lives, and the second one begins when you realize you only have one. When and how did your second life begin?

That's a very deep question. Most people who are past a certain age have had this feeling or phenomenon; they've gone through life a certain way and then gotten to a certain stage and had to make some pretty big changes. I'm definitely also in that boat.

I struggled for a lot of my life to have certain material and social successes. When I achieved those material and social successes (or at least was beyond a point where they didn't matter as much), I realized the people around me who had achieved similar successes and were on their way to achieving more didn't seem all that happy. In my case, there was definitely hedonic adaptation: I'd very quickly get used to anything.

This led me to the conclusion, which seems trite, that happiness is internal. That conclusion set me on a path of working more on my internal self and realizing all real success is internal and has very little to do with external circumstances.

One has to do the external thing anyway. We're biologically hard-wired. It's glib to say, "You can just turn it off." Your own life experience will bring you back to the internal path.

> The problem with getting good at a game, especially one with big rewards, is you continue playing it long after you should have outgrown it.
>
> Survival and replication drive put us on the work treadmill. Hedonic adaptation keeps us there. The trick is knowing when to jump off and play instead.

Who do you think of as successful?

Most people think of someone as successful when they win a game, whatever game they play themselves. If you're an athlete, you're going to think of a top athlete. If you're in business, you might think Elon Musk.

A few years ago, I would have said Steve Jobs, because he was part of the driving force creating something that changed lives for all of humanity. I think Marc Andreessen is successful, not because of his recent incarnation as a venture capitalist, but because of the incredible work he did with Netscape. Satoshi Nakamoto is successful in that he created Bitcoin, which is this incredible technological creation that will have repercussions for decades to come. Of course, Elon Musk, because he changed everyone's viewpoint on what is possible with modern technology and entrepreneurship. I consider those creators and commercializers successful.

To me, the real winners are the ones who step out of the game entirely, who don't even play the game, who rise above it. Those are the people who have such internal mental and self-control and self-awareness, they need nothing from anybody else. There are a couple of these characters I know in my life. Jerzy Gregorek—I would consider him successful because he doesn't need anything from anybody. He's at peace, he's healthy, and whether he makes more money or less money compared to the next person has no effect on his mental state.

Historically, I would say the legendary Buddha or Krishnamurti, whose stuff I like reading, they are successful in the sense that they step out of the game entirely. Winning or losing does not matter to them.

There's a line from Blaise Pascal I read. Basically, it says: "All of man's troubles arise because he cannot sit in a room quietly by himself." If you could just sit for thirty minutes and be happy, you are successful. That is a very powerful place to be, but very few of us get there.

I think of happiness as an emergent property of peace. If you're peaceful inside and out, that will eventually result in happiness. But peace is a very hard thing to come by. The irony is the way most of us try to find peace is through war. When you start a business, in a way, you're going to war. When you struggle with your roommates as to who should clean the dishes, you're going to war. You're struggling so you can have some sense of security and peace later.

In reality, peace is not a guarantee. It's always flowing. It's always changing. You want to learn the core skill set of flowing with life and accepting it in most cases.

> You can get almost anything you want out of life, as long as it's one thing and you want it far more than anything else.

In my own personal experience, the place I end up the most is wanting to be at peace.

Peace is happiness at rest, and happiness is peace in motion. You can convert peace into happiness anytime you want. But peace is what you want most of the time. If you're a peaceful person, anything you do will be a happy activity.

Today, the way we think you get peace is by resolving all your external problems. But there are unlimited external problems.

The only way to actually get peace on the inside is by giving up this idea of problems.

ENVY IS THE ENEMY OF HAPPINESS

I don't think life is that hard. I think we make it hard. One of the things I'm trying to get rid of is the word "should." Whenever the word "should" creeps up in your mind, it's guilt or social programming. Doing something because you "should" basically means you don't actually want to do it. It's just making you miserable, so I'm trying to eliminate as many "shoulds" from my life as possible.

> The enemy of peace of mind is expectations drilled into you by society and other people.

Socially, we're told, "Go work out. Go look good." That's a multiplayer competitive game. Other people can see if I'm doing a good job or not. We're told, "Go make money. Go buy a big house." Again, external multiplayer competitive game. Training yourself to be happy is completely internal. There is no external progress, no external validation. You're competing against yourself—it is a single-player game.

We're like bees or ants. We are such social creatures, we're externally programmed and driven. We don't know how to play and win these single-player games anymore. We compete purely in multiplayer games.

The reality is life is a single-player game. You're born alone. You're going to die alone. All of your interpretations are alone.

All your memories are alone. You're gone in three generations, and nobody cares. Before you showed up, nobody cared. It's all single player.

> Perhaps one reason why yoga and meditation are hard to sustain is they have no extrinsic value. Purely single-player games.

Buffett has a great example when he asks if you want to be the world's best lover and known as the worst, or the world's worst lover and known as the best? [paraphrased] in reference to an inner or external scorecard.

Exactly right. All the real scorecards are internal.

Jealousy was a very hard emotion for me to overcome. When I was young, I had a lot of jealousy. By and by, I learned to get rid of it. It still crops up every now and then. It's such a poisonous emotion because, at the end of the day, you're no better off with jealousy. You're unhappier, and the person you're jealous of is still successful or good-looking or whatever they are.

One day, I realized with all these people I was jealous of, I couldn't just choose little aspects of their life. I couldn't say I want his body, I want her money, I want his personality. You have to be that person. Do you want to actually be that person with all of their reactions, their desires, their family, their happiness level, their outlook on life, their self-image? If you're not willing to do a wholesale, 24/7, 100 percent swap with who that person is, then there is no point in being jealous.

Once I came to that realization, jealousy faded away because I don't want to be anybody else. I'm perfectly happy being me. By the way, even that is under my control. To be happy being me. It's just there are no social rewards for it.

HAPPINESS IS BUILT BY HABITS

My most surprising discovery in the last five years is that peace and happiness are skills. These are not things you are born with. Yes, there is a genetic range. And a lot of it is conditioning from your environment, but you can un-condition and recondition yourself.

You can increase your happiness over time, and it starts with believing you can do it.

It's a skill. Just like nutrition is a skill, dieting is a skill, working out is a skill, making money is a skill, meeting girls and guys is a skill, having good relationships is a skill, even love is a skill. It starts with realizing they're skills you can learn. When you put your intention and focus on it, the world can become a better place.

> When working, surround yourself with people more successful than you.
>
> When playing, surround yourself with people happier than you.

What type of skill is happiness?

It's all trial and error. You just see what works. You can try sitting meditation. Did that work for you? Was it Tantra meditation or was it Vipassana meditation? Was it a ten-day retreat or was twenty minutes enough?

Okay. None of those worked. But what if I tried yoga? What if I kite-surfed? What if I go car racing? What about cooking? Does that make me Zen? You literally have to try all of these things until you find something that works for you.

When it comes to medicines for the mind, the placebo effect is 100 percent effective. When it comes to your mind, you want to be positively inclined, not incredulous in belief. If it is fully internal, you should have a positive mindset.

For example, I was reading *The Power of Now* by Eckhart Tolle, which is a fantastic introduction to being present, for people who are not religious. He shows you the single-most important thing is to be present and hammers it home over and over again until you get it.

He wrote about this body-energy exercise. You lie down and you feel the energy moving around your body. At that point, the old me would have put the book down and said, "Well, that's BS." But the new me said, "Well, if I believe it, maybe it'll work." I went into it with a positive mindset. I laid down and tried the meditation. You know what? It felt really good.

How does someone build the skill of happiness?

You can build good habits. Not drinking alcohol will keep your mood more stable. Not eating sugar will keep your mood more stable. Not going on Facebook, Snapchat, or Twitter will keep your mood more stable. Playing video games will make you happier in the short run—and I used to be an avid gamer—but in the long run, it could ruin your happiness. You're being fed dopamine and having dopamine withdrawn from you in these little uncontrollable ways. Caffeine is another one where you trade long term for the short term.

Essentially, you have to go through your life replacing your thoughtless bad habits with good ones, making a commitment to be a happier person. At the end of the day, you are a combination of your habits and the people who you spend the most time with.

When we're kids, we have very few habits. Over time, we learn the things we are not supposed to do. We become self-conscious. We start forming habits and routines.

Many distinctions between people who get happier as they get older and people who don't can be explained by what habits they have developed. Are they habits that will increase your long-term happiness rather than your short-term happiness? Are you surrounding yourself with people who are generally positive and upbeat people? Are those relationships low-maintenance? Do you admire and respect but not envy them?

There's the "five chimps theory" where you can predict a chimp's behavior by the five chimps it hangs out with the most. I think that applies to humans as well. Maybe it's politically incorrect to say you should choose your friends very wisely. But you shouldn't choose them haphazardly based on who you live next to or who you happen to work with. The people who are the most happy and optimistic choose the right five chimps.

The first rule of handling conflict is: Don't hang around people who constantly engage in conflict. I'm not interested in anything unsustainable or even hard to sustain, including difficult relationships.

> If you can't see yourself working with someone for life, don't work with them for a day.

There's a friend of mine, a Persian guy named Behzad. He just loves life, and he has no time for anybody who is not happy.

If you ask Behzad what's his secret? He'll just look up and say, "Stop asking why and start saying wow." The world is such an amazing place. As humans, we're used to taking everything for granted. Like what you and I are doing right now. We're sitting indoors, wearing clothes, well-fed, and communicating with each other through space and time. We should be two monkeys sitting in the jungle right now watching the sun going down, asking ourselves where we are going to sleep.

When we get something, we assume the world owes it to us. If you're present, you'll realize how many gifts and how much abundance there is around us at all times. That's all you really need to do. I'm here now, and I have all these incredible things at my disposal.

The most important trick to being happy is to realize happiness is a skill you develop and a choice you make. You choose to be happy, and then you work at it. It's just like building muscles. It's just like losing weight. It's just like succeeding at your job. It's just like learning calculus.

You decide it's important to you. You prioritize it above everything else. You read everything on the topic.

HAPPINESS HABITS

I have a series of tricks I use to try and be happier in the moment. At first, they were silly and difficult and required a lot of attention, but now some of them have become second nature. By doing them religiously, I've managed to increase my happiness level quite a bit.

The obvious one is meditation—insight meditation. Working toward a specific purpose on it, which is to try and understand how my mind works.

Just being very aware in every moment. If I catch myself judging somebody, I can stop myself and say, "What's the positive interpretation of this?" I used to get annoyed about things. Now I always look for the positive side of it. It used to take a rational effort. It used to take a few seconds for me to come up with a positive. Now I can do it sub-second.

I try to get more sunlight on my skin. I look up and smile.

Every time you catch yourself desiring something, say, "Is it so important to me I'll be unhappy unless this goes my way?" You're going to find with the vast majority of things it's just not true.

I think dropping caffeine made me happier. It makes me more of a stable person.

I think working out every day made me happier. If you have peace of body, it's easier to have peace of mind.

The more you judge, the more you separate yourself. You'll feel good for an instant, because you feel good about yourself, thinking you're better than someone. Later, you're going to feel lonely. Then, you see negativity everywhere. The world just reflects your own feelings back at you.

Tell your friends you're a happy person. Then, you'll be forced to conform to it. You'll have a consistency bias. You have to live up to it. Your friends will expect you to be a happy person.

Recover time and happiness by minimizing your use of these three smartphone apps: phone, calendar, and alarm clock.

The more secrets you have, the less happy you're going to be.

Caught in a funk? Use meditation, music, and exercise to reset your mood. Then choose a new path to commit emotional energy for rest of day.

Hedonic adaptation is more powerful for man-made things (cars, houses, clothes, money) than for natural things (food, sex, exercise).

No exceptions—all screen activities linked to less happiness, all non-screen activities linked to more happiness.

A personal metric: how much of the day is spent doing things out of obligation rather than out of interest?

It's the news' job to make you anxious and angry. But its underlying scientific, economic, education, and conflict trends are positive. Stay optimistic.

Politics, academia, and social status are all zero-sum games. Positive-sum games create positive people.

Increase serotonin in the brain without drugs: Sunlight, exercise, positive thinking, and tryptophan.

CHANGING HABITS:

Pick one thing. Cultivate a desire. Visualize it.

Plan a sustainable path.

Identify needs, triggers, and substitutes.

Tell your friends.

Track meticulously.

Self-discipline is a bridge to a new self-image.

Bake in the new self-image. It's who you are—now.

> First, you know it. Then, you understand it. Then, you can explain it. Then, you can feel it. Finally, you are it.

FIND HAPPINESS IN ACCEPTANCE

In any situation in life, you always have three choices: you can change it, you can accept it, or you can leave it.

If you want to change it, then it is a desire. It will cause you suffering until you successfully change it. So don't pick too many of those. Pick one big desire in your life at any given time to give yourself purpose and motivation.

Why not two?

You'll be distracted.

Even one is hard enough. Being peaceful comes from having your mind clear of thoughts. And a lot of clarity comes from being in the present moment. It's very hard to be in the present moment if you're thinking, "I need to do this. I want that. This has got to change."

You always have three options: you can change it, you can accept it, or you can leave it. What is not a good option is to sit around wishing you would change it but not changing it, wishing you could leave it but not leaving it and not accepting it. That struggle or aversion is responsible for most of our misery. The phrase I probably use the most to myself in my head is just one word: "accept."

What does acceptance look like to you?

It's to be okay whatever the outcome is. It's to be balanced and centered. It's to step back and to see the grander scheme of things.

We don't always get what we want, but sometimes what is happening is for the best. The sooner you can accept it as a reality, the sooner you can adapt to it.

Achieving acceptance is very difficult. I have a couple of hacks I try, but I wouldn't say they are totally successful.

One hack is stepping back and looking at previous bits of suffering I've had in my life. I write them down. "Last time you broke up with somebody, last time you had a business failure, last time you had a health issue, what happened?" I can trace the growth and improvement that came from it years later.

I have another hack I use for minor annoyances. When they happen, a part of me will instantly react negatively. But I've learned to mentally ask myself, "What is the positive of this situation?"

"Okay, I'll be late for a meeting. But what is the benefit to me? I get to relax and watch the birds for a moment. I'll also spend less time in that boring meeting." There's almost always something positive.

Even if you can't come up with something positive, you can say, "Well, the Universe is going to teach me something now. Now I get to listen and learn."

To give you the simplest example: I was at an event and afterward, someone flooded my inbox with a whole bunch of photos they took.

There was a tiny instant judgment saying, "Come on, couldn't you have just selected a few of the best? Who sends a hundred photos?" But then immediately I asked myself, "What is the positive?" The positive is that I get to pick my five favorite photos. I get to use my judgment.

Over the last year, by practicing this hack enough, I've managed to go from taking a couple of seconds to think of a response, to now my brain doing it almost instantaneously. That's a habit you can train yourself to do.

How do you learn to accept things you can't change?

Fundamentally, it boils down to one big hack: embracing death.

Death is the most important thing that is ever going to happen to you. When you look at your death and you acknowledge it, rather than running away from it, it'll bring great meaning to your life. We spend so much of our life trying to avoid death. So much of what we struggle for can be classified as a quest for immortality.

If you're religious and believe there is an afterlife, then you'll be taken care of. If you're not religious, maybe you'll have kids. If you're an artist, a painter, or a businessman, you want to leave a legacy behind.

Here's a hot tip: There is no legacy. There's nothing to leave. We're all going to be gone. Our children will be gone. Our works will be dust. Our civilizations will be dust. Our planet will be dust. Our solar system will be dust. In the grand scheme of things, the Universe has been around for ten billion years. It'll be around for another ten billion years.

Your life is a firefly blink in a night. You're here for such a brief period of time. If you fully acknowledge the futility of what you're doing, then I think it can bring great happiness and peace because you realize this is a game. But it's a fun game. All that matters is you experience your reality as you go through life. Why not interpret it in the most positive possible way?

Any moment where you're not having a great time, when you're not really happy, you're not doing anyone any favors. It's not like your unhappiness makes them better off somehow. All you're doing is wasting this incredibly small and precious time you have on this Earth. Keeping death on the forefront and not denying it is very important.

Whenever I get caught up in my ego battles, I just think of entire civilizations that have come and gone. For example, take the Sumerians. I'm sure they were important people and did great things, but go ahead and name me a single Sumerian. Tell me anything interesting or important Sumerians did that lasted. Nothing.

So maybe ten thousand years from now or a hundred thousand years from now, people will say, "Oh yeah, Americans. I've heard of Americans."

You're going to die one day, and none of this is going to matter. So enjoy yourself. Do something positive. Project some love. Make someone happy. Laugh a little bit. Appreciate the moment. And do your work.

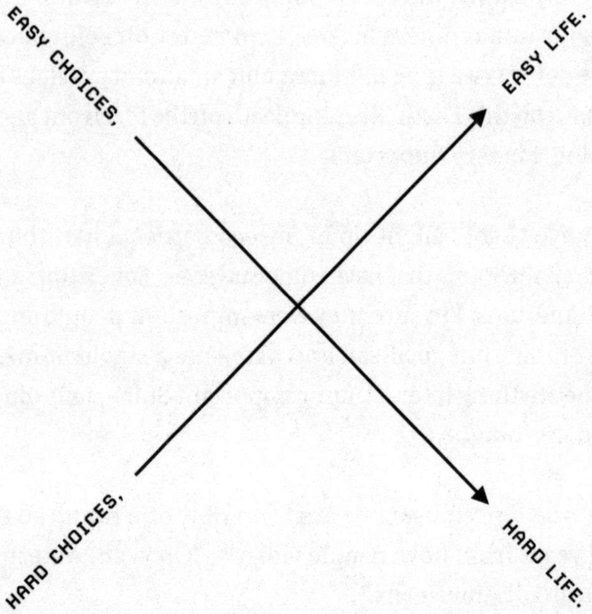
EASY CHOICES,
EASY LIFE.
HARD CHOICES,
HARD LIFE.

I SAVING YOURSELF

Doctors won't make you healthy.
Nutritionists won't make you slim.
Teachers won't make you smart.
Gurus won't make you calm.
Mentors won't make you rich.
Trainers won't make you fit.

Ultimately, you have to take responsibility.

Save yourself.

CHOOSING TO BE YOURSELF

A lot of what goes on today is what many of you are doing right now—beating yourself up and scribbling notes and saying, "I need to do this, and I need to do that, and I need to do..." No, you don't need to do anything.

All you should do is what you want to do. If you stop trying to figure out how to do things the way other people want you to do them, you get to listen to the little voice inside your head that wants to do things a certain way. Then, you get to be you.

> I never met my greatest mentor. I wanted so much to be like him. But his message was the opposite: Be yourself, with passionate intensity.

No one in the world is going to beat you at being you. You're never going to be as good at being me as I am. I'm never going to be as good at being you as you are. Certainly, listen and absorb, but don't try to emulate. It's a fool's errand. Instead, each person is uniquely qualified at something. They have some specific knowledge, capability, and desire nobody else in the world does, purely from the combinatorics of human DNA and development.

> The combinatorics of human DNA and experience are staggering. You will never meet any two humans who are substitutable for each other.

Your goal in life is to find the people, business, project, or art that needs you the most. There is something out there just for you. What you don't want to do is build checklists and decision frameworks built on what other people are doing. You're never going to be them. You'll never be good at being somebody else.

> To make an original contribution, you have to be irrationally obsessed with something.

CHOOSING TO CARE FOR YOURSELF

My number one priority in life, above my happiness, above my family, above my work, is my own health. It starts with my physical health. Second, it's my mental health. Third, it's my spiritual health. Then, it's my family's health. Then, it's my family's wellbeing. After that, I can go out and do whatever I need to do with the rest of the world.

> Nothing like a health problem to turn up the contrast dial for the rest of life.

What about the modern world steers us away from the way humans are meant to live?

There are many, many things.

There are a number on the physical side. We have diets we are not evolved to eat. A correct diet should probably look closer to a paleo diet, mostly eating vegetables with a small amount of meat and berries.

In terms of exercise, we're probably meant to play instead of running on a treadmill. We're probably evolved to use all of our five senses equally as opposed to favoring the visual cortex. In modern society, almost all of our inputs and communication are visual. We're not meant to walk in shoes. A lot of back and foot problems come from shoes. We're not meant to have clothes keep us warm all of the time. We're meant to have some cold exposure. It kickstarts your immune system.

We're not evolved to live in a perfectly sterile and clean environment. It leads to allergies and an untrained immune system. This is known as the hygiene hypothesis. We're evolved to live in much smaller tribes and to have more family around us. I partially grew up in India, and in India, everybody is in your business. There's a cousin, an aunt, an uncle who is in your face, which makes it hard to be depressed, because you are never alone. (I'm not referring to people with chemical depression. I'm talking more about the existential angst and malaise teenagers seem to go through.) But on the other hand, you have no privacy, so you can't be free. There are trade-offs.

We're not meant to check our phone every five minutes. The constant mood swings of getting a "like" then an angry comment makes us into anxious creatures. We evolved for scarcity but live in abundance. There's a constant struggle to say no when your genes always want to say yes. Yes to sugar. Yes to staying in this relationship. Yes to alcohol. Yes to drugs. Yes, yes, yes. Our bodies don't know how to say no.

> When everyone is sick, we no longer consider it a disease.

DIET

> Outside of math, physics, and chemistry, there isn't much "settled science." We're still arguing over what the optimal diet is.

Do you have an opinion on the ketogenic diet?

It seems really difficult to follow. It makes sense for the brain and the body to have a backup mechanism. For example, in the Ice Ages, humans evolved without many plants available. At the same time, we have been eating plants for thousands of years...I don't think plants are bad for you, but something closer to the paleo diet is probably correct.

I think the interplay between sugar and fat is really interesting. Fat is what makes you satiated. Fatty foods make you feel full. The easiest way to feel full is to go on a ketogenic diet, where you're eating tons of bacon all the time, and you're going to feel almost nauseous and not want to look at fat anymore.

Sugar makes you hungry. Sugar signals to your body, "There's this incredible food resource in the environment we're not evolved for," so you rush out to get sugar. The problem is the sugar effect dominates the fat effect. If you eat a fatty meal and you throw some sugar in, the sugar is going to deliver hunger and fat is going to deliver the calories and you're just going to binge. That's why all desserts are large combinations of fat and carbs together.

In nature, it's very rare to find carbs and fat together. In nature, I find carbs and fat together in coconuts, in mangoes, maybe in bananas, but it's basically tropical fruits. The combination of sugar and fat together is really deadly. You've got to watch out for that in your diet.

I'm not an expert, and the problem is diet and nutrition are like politics: everybody thinks they're an expert. Their identity is wrapped up in it because what they've been eating or what they think they should be eating is obviously the correct answer. Everybody has a little religion—it's just a really difficult topic to talk about. I will just say in general, any sensible diet avoids the combination of sugar and fat together.

> Dietary fat drives satiety. Dietary sugar drives hunger. The sugar effect dominates. Control your appetite accordingly.

Most fit and healthy people focus much more on what they eat than how much. Quality control is easier than (and leads to) quantity control.

Ironically, fasting (from a low-carb/paleo base) is easier than portion control. Once the body detects food, it overrides the brain.

What I wonder about Wonder Bread is how it can stay soft at room temperature for months. If bacteria won't eat it, should you?

It has been five thousand years, and we're still arguing over whether meat is poisonous or plants are poisonous. Ditch the extremists and any food invented in the last few hundred years.

When it comes to medicine and nutrition, subtract before you add.

My trainer sends me photos of his meals, and it reminds me we are all flavor addicts.

> World's simplest diet: The more processed the food, the less one should consume.

EXERCISE

> The harder the workout, the easier the day.

What habit would you say most positively impacts your life?

The daily morning workout. That has been a complete game-changer. It's made me feel healthier, younger. It's made me not go out late. It came from one simple thing, which is everybody says, "I don't have time." Basically, whenever you throw any so-called good habit at somebody, they'll have an excuse for themselves. Usually the most common is "I don't have time." "I don't have time" is just another way of saying "It's not a priority." What you really have to do is say whether it is a priority or not. If something is your number one priority, then you will do it. That's just the way life works. If you've got a fuzzy basket of ten or fifteen different priorities, you're going to end up getting none of them.

What I did was decide my number one priority in life, above my happiness, above my family, above my work, is my own health. It starts with my physical health. Because my physical health became my number one priority, then I could never say I don't have time. In the morning, I work out, and however long it takes is how long it takes. I do not start my day until I've worked out. I don't care if the world is imploding and melting down, it can wait another thirty minutes until I'm done working out.

It's pretty much every day. There are a few days where I've had to take a break because I'm traveling, or I'm injured or sick or something. I can count on one hand the number of breaks I take every year.

> One month of consistent yoga and I feel 10 years younger. To stay flexible is to stay young.

How you make a habit doesn't matter. Do something every day. It almost doesn't matter what you do. The people who are obsessing over whether to do weight training, tennis, Pilates, the high-intensity interval training method, "The Happy Body," or whatever. They're missing the point. The important thing is to do something every day. It doesn't matter what it is. The best workout for you is one you're excited enough to do every day.

> Walking meetings:
> - Brain works better
> - Exercise & sunlight
> - Shorter, less pleasantries
> - More dialogue, less monologue
> - No slides
> - End easily by walking back

Like everything in life, if you are willing to make the short-term sacrifice, you'll have the long-term benefit. My physical trainer

(Jerzy Gregorek) is a really wise, brilliant guy. He always says, "Easy choices, hard life. Hard choices, easy life."

Basically, if you are making the hard choices right now in what to eat, you're not eating all the junk food you want, and making the hard choice to work out. So, your life long-term will be easy. You won't be sick. You won't be unhealthy. The same is true of values. The same is true of saving up for a rainy day. The same is true of how you approach your relationships. **If you make the easy choices right now, your overall life will be a lot harder.**

MEDITATION
IS

INTERMITTENT
FASTING

FOR THE MIND.

> An emotion is our evolved biology predicting the future impact of a current event. In modern settings, it's usually exaggerated or wrong.

Why is meditation so powerful?

Your breath is one of the few places where your autonomic nervous system meets your voluntary nervous system. It's involuntary, but you can also control it.

I think a lot of meditation practices put an emphasis on the breath because it is a gateway into your autonomic nervous system. There are many, many cases in the medical and spiritual literature of people controlling their bodies at levels that should be autonomous.

Your mind is such a powerful thing. What's so unusual about your forebrain sending signals to your hindbrain and your hindbrain routing resources to your entire body?

You can do it just by breathing. Relaxed breathing tells your body you're safe. Then, your forebrain doesn't need as many resources as it normally does. Now, the extra energy can be sent to your hindbrain, and it can reroute those resources to the rest of your body.

I'm not saying you can beat whatever illness you have just because you activated your hindbrain. But you're devoting most of the energy normally required to care about the external environment to the immune system.

I highly recommend listening to *The Tim Ferris Show* with Wim Hof. He is a walking miracle. Wim's nickname is the Ice Man. He holds the world record for the longest time spent in an ice bath and swimming in freezing cold water. I was very inspired by him, not only because he's capable of super-human physical feats, but because he does it while being incredibly kind and happy—which is not easy to accomplish.

He advocates cold exposure, because he believes people are too separate from their natural environment. We're constantly clothed, fed, and warm. Our bodies have lost touch with the cold. The cold is important because it can activate the immune system.

So, he advocates taking long ice baths. Being from the Indian subcontinent, I'm strongly against the idea of ice baths. But Wim inspired me to give cold showers a try. And I did so by using the Wim Hof breathing method. It involves hyperventilating to get more oxygen into your blood, which raises your core temperature. Then, you can go into the shower.

The first few cold showers were hilarious because I'd slowly ease myself in, wincing the entire way. I started about four or five months ago. Now, I turn the shower on full-blast, and then I walk right in. I don't give myself any time to hesitate. As soon as I hear the voice in my head telling me how cold it's going to be, I know I have to walk in.

I learned a very important lesson from this: most of our suffering comes from avoidance. Most of the suffering from a cold shower is the tip-toeing your way in. Once you're in, you're in. It's not suffering. It's just cold. Your body saying it's cold is different than your mind saying it's cold. Acknowledge your body saying it's cold. Look at it. Deal with it. Accept it, but don't mentally suffer over it. Taking a cold shower for two minutes isn't going to kill you.

Having a cold shower helps you re-learn that lesson every morning. Now hot showers are just one less thing I need out of life.

> Meditation is intermittent fasting for the mind.
>
> Too much sugar leads to a heavy body, and too many distractions lead to a heavy mind.
>
> Time spent undistracted and alone, in self-examination, journaling, meditation, resolves the unresolved and takes us from mentally fat to fit.

Do you have a current meditation practice?

I think meditation is like dieting, where everyone is supposedly following a regimen. Everyone says they do it, but nobody actually does it. The real set of people who meditate on a regular basis, I've found, are pretty rare. I've identified and tried at least four different forms of meditation.

The one I found works best for me is called Choiceless Awareness, or Nonjudgmental Awareness. As you're going about your daily business (hopefully, there's some nature) and you're not talking to anybody else, you practice learning to accept the moment you're in without making judgments. You don't think, "Oh, there's a homeless guy over there, better cross the street" or look at someone running by and say, "He's out of shape, and I'm in better shape than him."

If I saw a guy with a bad hair day, I would at first think "Haha, he has a bad hair day." Well, why am I laughing at him to make me feel better about myself? And why am I trying to make me feel better about my own hair? Because I'm losing my hair, and I'm afraid it's going to go away. What I find is 90 percent of thoughts I have are fear-based. The other 10 percent may be desire-based.

You don't make any decisions. You don't judge anything. You just accept everything. If I do that for ten or fifteen minutes while walking around, I end up in a very peaceful, grateful state. Choiceless Awareness works well for me.

You could also do transcendental meditation, which is where you're using repetitive chanting to create a white noise in your head to bury your thoughts. Or, you can just very keenly and very alertly be aware of your thoughts as they happen. As you watch your thoughts, you realize how many of them are fear-based. The moment you recognize a fear, without even trying it goes away. After a while, your mind quiets.

When your mind quiets, you stop taking everything around you for granted. You start to notice the details. You think, "Wow, I live in such a beautiful place. It's so great that I have clothes, and I can go to Starbucks and get a coffee anytime. Look at these people—each one has a perfectly valid and complete life going on in their own heads."

It pops us out of the story we're constantly telling ourselves. If you stop talking to yourself for even ten minutes, if you stop obsessing over your own story, you'll realize we are really far up Maslow's hierarchy of needs, and life is pretty good.

> Life-hack: When in bed, meditate. Either you will have a deep meditation or fall asleep. Victory either way.

Another method I've learned is to just sit there and you close your eyes for at least one hour a day. You surrender to whatever happens—don't make any effort whatsoever. You make no effort for something, and you make no effort against anything. If there are thoughts running through your mind, you let the thoughts run.

For your entire life, things have been happening to you. Some good, some bad, most of which you have processed and dissolved, but a few stuck with you. Over time, more and more stuck with you, and they almost became like these barnacles stuck to you.

You lost your childhood sense of wonder and of being present and happy. You lost your inner happiness because you built up this personality of unresolved pain, errors, fears, and desires that glommed onto you like a bunch of barnacles.

How do you get those barnacles off you? What happens in meditation is you're sitting there and not resisting your mind. These things will start bubbling up. It's like a giant inbox of unanswered emails, going back to your childhood. They will come out one by one, and you will be forced to deal with them.

You will be forced to resolve them. Resolving them doesn't take any work—you just observe them. Now you're an adult with some distance, time, and space from previous events, and you can just resolve them. You can be much more objective about how you view them.

Over time, you will resolve a lot of these deep-seated unresolved things you have in your mind. Once they're resolved, there will come a day when you sit down to meditate, and you'll hit a mental "inbox zero." When you open your mental "email" and there are none, that is a pretty amazing feeling.

It's a state of joy and bliss and peace. Once you have it, you don't want to give it up. If you can get a free hour of bliss every morning just by sitting and closing your eyes, that is worth its weight in gold. It will change your life.

I recommend meditating one hour each morning because anything less is not enough time to really get deep into it. I would recommend if you really want to try meditation, try sixty days of one hour a day, first thing in the morning. After about sixty days, you will be tired of listening to your own mind. You will have resolved a lot of issues, or you have heard them enough to see through those fears and issues.

Meditation isn't hard. All you have to do is sit there and do nothing. Just sit down. Close your eyes and say, "I'm just going to give myself a break for an hour. This is my hour off from life. This is the hour I'm not going to do anything.

"If thoughts come, thoughts come. I'm not going to fight them. I'm not going to embrace them. I'm not going to think harder about them. I'm not going to reject them. I'm just going to sit here for an hour with my eyes closed, and I'm going to do nothing." How hard is that? Why can you not do anything for an hour? What's so hard about giving yourself an hour-long break?

Was there a moment you realized you could control how you interpreted things? I think one problem people have is not recognizing they can control how they interpret and respond to a situation.

I think everyone knows it's possible. There's a great Osho lecture, titled "The Attraction for Drugs Is Spiritual." He talks about why do people do drugs (everything from alcohol to psychedelics to cannabis). They're doing it to control their mental state. They're doing it to control how they react. Some people drink because it helps them not care as much, or they're potheads because they can zone out, or they do psychedelics to feel very present or connected to nature. The attraction of drugs is spiritual.

All of society does this to some extent. People chasing thrills in action sports or flow states or orgasms—any of these states people strive for are people trying to get out of their own heads. They're trying to get away from the voice in their heads—the overdeveloped sense of self.

At the very least, I do not want my sense of self to continue to develop and strengthen as I get older. I want it to be weaker and more muted so I can be more in present everyday reality, accept nature and the world for what it is, and appreciate it very much as a child would.

The first thing to realize is you can observe your mental state. Meditation doesn't mean you're suddenly going to gain the superpower to control your internal state. The advantage of meditation is recognizing just how out of control your mind is. It is like a monkey flinging feces, running around the room, making trouble, shouting, and breaking things. It's completely uncontrollable. It's an out-of-control madperson.

You have to see this mad creature in operation before you feel a certain distaste toward it and start separating yourself from it. In that separation is liberation. You realize, "Oh, I don't want to be that person. Why am I so out of control?" Awareness alone calms you down.

> Insight meditation lets you run your brain in debug mode until you realize you're just a subroutine in a larger program.

I try to keep an eye on my internal monologue. It doesn't always work. In the computer programming sense, I try to run my brain in "debugging mode" as much as possible. When I'm talking to someone, or when I'm engaged in a group activity, it's almost impossible because your brain has too many things to handle. If I'm by myself, like just this morning, I'm brushing my teeth and I start thinking forward to a podcast. I started going through this little fantasy where I imagined Shane asking me a bunch of questions and I was fantasy- answering them. Then, I caught myself. I put my brain in debug mode and just watched every little instruction go by.

I said, "Why am I fantasy-future planning? Why can't I just stand here and brush my teeth?" It's the awareness my brain was running off in the future and planning some fantasy scenario out of ego. I was like, "Well, do I really care if I embarrass myself? Who cares? I'm going to die anyway. This is all going to go to zero, and I won't remember anything, so this is pointless."

Then, I shut down, and I went back to brushing my teeth. I was noticing how good the toothbrush was and how good it felt. Then the next moment, I'm off to thinking something else. I have to look at my brain again and say, "Do I really need to solve this problem right now?"

Ninety-five percent of what my brain runs off and tries to do, I don't need to tackle in that exact moment. If the brain is like a muscle, I'll be better off resting it, being at peace. When a particular problem arises, I'll immerse myself in it.

Right now as we're talking, I'd rather dedicate myself to being completely lost in the conversation and to being 100 percent focused on this as opposed to thinking about "Oh, when I brushed my teeth, did I do it the right way?"

The ability to singularly focus is related to the ability to lose yourself and be present, happy, and (ironically) more effective.

It's almost like you're taking yourself out of a certain frame and you're watching things from a different perspective even though you're in your own mind.

Buddhists talk about awareness versus the ego. They're really talking about how you can think of your brain, your consciousness, as a multilayered mechanism. There's a core-base, kernel-level OS running. Then, there are applications running on top. (I like to think of it as computer and geek speak.)

I'm actually going back to my awareness level of OS, which is always calm, always peaceful, and generally happy and content. I'm trying to stay in awareness mode and not activate the monkey mind, which is always worried, frightened, and anxious. It serves incredible purpose, but I try not to activate the monkey mind until I need it. When I need it, I want to just focus on that. If I run it 24/7, I waste energy and the monkey mind becomes me. I am more than my monkey mind.

Another thing: spirituality, religion, Buddhism, or anything you follow will teach you over time you are more than just your mind. You are more than just your habits. You are more than just your preferences. You're a level of awareness. You're a body. Modern humans, we don't live enough in our bodies. We don't live enough in our awareness. We live too much in this internal monologue in our heads. All of which is just programmed into you by society and by the environment when you were younger.

You are basically a bunch of DNA that reacted to environmental effects when you were younger. You recorded the good and bad experiences, and you use them to prejudge everything thrown against you. Then you're using those experiences, constantly trying and predict and change the future.

As you get older, the sum of preferences you've accumulated is very, very large. These habitual reactions end up as runaway freight trains controlling your mood. We should control our own moods. Why don't we study how to control our moods? What a masterful thing it would be if you could say, "Right now I would like to be in the curious state," and then you can genuinely get yourself into the curious state. Or say, "I want to be in a mourning state. I'm mourning a loved one, and I want to grieve for them. I really want to feel that. I don't want to be distracted by a computer programming problem due tomorrow."

The mind itself is a muscle—it can be trained and conditioned. It has been haphazardly conditioned by society to be out of our control. If you look at your mind with awareness and intent (a 24/7 job you're working at every moment) I think you can unpack your own mind, your emotions, thoughts, and reactions. Then you can start reconfiguring. You can start rewriting this program to what you want.

> Meditation is turning off society and listening to yourself.
>
> It only "works" when done for its own sake.
>
> Hiking is walking meditation.
>
> Journaling is writing meditation.
>
> Praying is gratitude meditation.
>
> Showering is accidental meditation.
>
> Sitting quietly is direct meditation.

CHOOSING TO BUILD YOURSELF

> The greatest superpower is the ability to change yourself.

What's the biggest mistake you've made in your life and how did you recover?

I've made a class of mistakes I would summarize the same way. The mistakes were obvious only in hindsight through one exercise, which is asking yourself: when you're thirty, what advice would you give your twenty-year-old self? And when you're forty, what advice would you give your thirty-year-old self? (Maybe if you're younger, you can do it by every five years.) Sit down and say, "Okay, 2007, what was I doing? How was I feeling? 2008, what was I doing? How was I feeling? 2009, what was I doing? How was I feeling?"

Life is going to play out the way it's going to play out. There will be some good and some bad. Most of it is actually just up to your interpretation. You're born, you have a set of sensory experiences, and then you die. How you choose to interpret those experiences is up to you, and different people interpret them in different ways.

Really, I wish I had done all of the same things, but with less emotion and less anger. The most celebrated example would be when I was younger, I started a company. This company did well, but I didn't do well, so I sued some of the people involved. It was a good outcome for me in the end, and everything worked out okay, but there was a lot of angst and a lot of anger.

Today, I wouldn't have the angst and the anger. I would have just walked up to the people and said, "Look, this is what happened. This is what I'm going to do. This is how I'm going to do it. This is what's fair. This is what's not."

I would have realized the anger and emotions are a huge, completely unnecessary consequence. Now, I'm trying to learn from that and do the same things I think are the right things to do but without anger and with a very long-term point of view. If you take a very long-term point of view and take the emotion out of it, I wouldn't consider those things mistakes anymore.

Again, habits are everything—everything we are. We are trained in habits from when we are children, including potty training, when to cry and when not to, how to smile and when not to. These things become habits—behaviors we learn and integrate into ourselves.

When we're older, we're a collection of thousands of habits constantly running subconsciously. We have a little bit of extra brainpower in our neocortex for solving new problems. You become your habits.

This came to light for me when my trainer gave me a routine to do every single day. I had never worked out every single day before. It's a light workout. It's not tough on your body, but I did this workout every single day. I realized the incredible, astonishing transformation it had on me both physically and mentally.

> To have peace of mind, you have to have peace of body first.

This taught me the power of habits. I started realizing it's all about habits. At any given time, I'm either trying to pick up a good habit or discard a previous bad habit. It takes time.

If someone says, "I want to be fit, I want to be healthy. Right now, I'm out of shape and I'm fat." Well, nothing sustainable is going to work for you in three months. It's going to be at least a ten-year journey. Every six months (depending on how fast you can do it), you're going to break bad habits and pick up good habits.

One of the things Krishnamurti talks about is being in an internal state of revolution. You should always be internally ready for a complete change. Whenever we say we're going to *try* to do something or *try* to form a habit, we're wimping out.

We're just saying to ourselves, "I'm going to buy myself some more time." The reality is when our emotions want us to do something, we just do it. If you want to go approach a pretty girl, if you want to have a drink, if you really desire something, you just go do it.

When you say, "I'm *going to* do this," and "I'm *going to be* that," you're really putting it off. You're giving yourself an out. At least if you're self-aware, you can think, "'I say I want to do this, but I don't really because if I really wanted to do it, I would just do it."

Commit externally to enough people. For example, if you want to quit smoking, all you have to do is go to everybody you know and say, "I quit smoking. I did it. I give you my word."

That's all you need to do. Go ahead, right? But most of us say we're not quite ready. We know we don't want to commit ourselves externally. It's important to be honest with yourself and say, "Okay, I'm not ready to give up smoking. I like it too much, it is going to be too hard for me to give up."

Say instead, "I'll set a more reasonable goal for myself; I'll cut down to the following amount. I can commit to that externally. I'm going to work on that for three or six months. When I get there, I'll take the next step, as opposed to beating myself up over it."

When you really want to change, you just change. But most of us don't really want to change—we don't want to go through the pain just yet. At least recognize it, be aware of it, and give yourself a smaller change you can actually carry out.

> Impatience with actions, patience with results.

Anything you have to do, just get it done. Why wait? You're not getting any younger. Your life is slipping away. You don't want to spend it waiting in line. You don't want to spend it traveling back and forth. You don't want to spend it doing things you know ultimately aren't part of your mission.

When you do them, you want to do them as quickly as you can while doing them well with your full attention. But then, you just have to be patient with the results because you're dealing with complex systems and many people.

It takes a long time for markets to adopt products. It takes time for people to get comfortable working with each other. It takes time for great products to emerge as you polish away, polish away, polish away. Impatience with actions, patience with results. As Nivi said, inspiration is perishable. When you have inspiration, act on it right then and there.

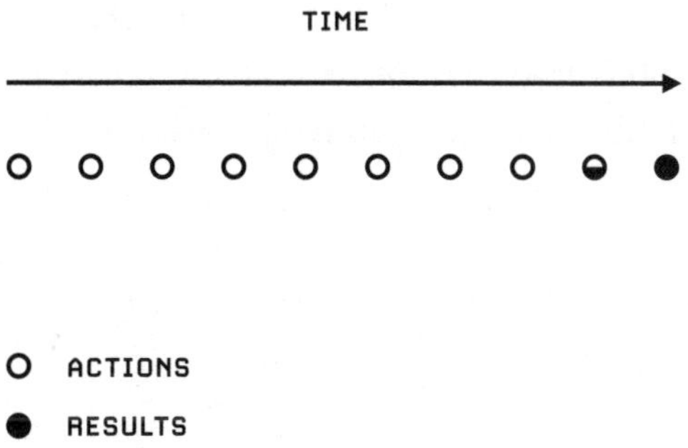

CHOOSING TO GROW YOURSELF

I don't believe in specific goals. Scott Adams famously said, "Set up systems, not goals." Use your judgment to figure out what kinds of environments you can thrive in, and then create an environment around you so you're statistically likely to succeed.

> The current environment programs the brain, but the clever brain can choose its upcoming environment.

I'm not going to be the most successful person on the planet, nor do I want to be. I just want to be the most successful version of myself while working the least hard possible. I want to live in a way that if my life played out 1,000 times, Naval is successful 999 times. He's not a billionaire, but he does pretty well each time. He may not have nailed life in every regard, but he sets up systems so he's failed in very few places.

Remember I started as a poor kid in India, right? If I can make it, anybody can, in that sense. Obviously, I had all my limbs, my mental faculties, and I did have an education. There are some prerequisites you can't get past. But if you're reading this book, you probably have the requisite means at your disposal, which is a functioning body and a functioning mind.

> If there's something you want to do later, do it now. There is no "later."

How do you personally learn about new subjects?

Mostly, I just stay on the basics. Even when I learn physics or science, I stick to the basics. I read concepts for fun. I'm more likely to do something that has arithmetic in it than calculus. I won't be a great physicist at this point. Maybe in the next lifetime or my kid will do it, but it's too late for me. I have to stick to what I enjoy.

Science is, to me, the study of truth. It is the only true discipline because it makes falsifiable predictions. It actually changes the world. Applied science becomes technology, and technology is what separates us from the animals and allows us to have things like cell phones, houses, cars, heat, and electricity.

Science, to me, is the study of truth and mathematics is the language of science and nature.

I'm not religious, but I'm spiritual. To me, that is the most devotional thing that I could do, to study the laws of the Universe. The same kick that someone might get out of being in Mecca or Medina and bowing to the prophet, I get the same feeling of awe and small sense of self when I study science. For me, it's unparalleled and I'd rather stay at the basics. This is the beauty of reading.

Do you agree with the idea "If you read what everybody else is reading, you're going to think what everyone else is thinking"?

I think almost everything that people read these days is designed for social approval.

I know people who have read one hundred regurgitated books on evolution and they've never read Darwin. Think of the number of macroeconomists out there. I think most of them have read tons of treatises in economics but haven't read any Adam Smith.

At some level, you're doing it for social approval. You're doing it to fit in with the other monkeys. You're fitting in to get along with the herd. That's not where the returns are in life. The returns in life are being out of the herd.

Social approval is inside the herd. If you want social approval, definitely go read what the herd is reading. It takes a level of contrarianism to say, "Nope. I'm just going to do my own thing. Regardless of the social outcome, I will learn anything I think is interesting."

Do you think there's some loss aversion there? Because once you diverge, you're not sure if you're diverging toward a positive outcome or a negative outcome?

Absolutely. I think that's why the smartest and the most successful people I know started out as losers. If you view yourself as a loser, as someone who was cast out by society and has no role in normal society, then you will do your own thing and you're much more likely to find a winning path. It helps to start out by saying, "I'm never going to be popular. I'm never going to be accepted. I'm already a loser. I'm not going to get what all the other kids have. I've just got to be happy being me."

> For self-improvement without self-discipline, update your self-image.

Everyone's motivated at something. It just depends on the thing. Even the people that we say are unmotivated are suddenly really motivated when they're playing video games. I think motivation is relative, so you just have to find the thing you're into.

> Grind and sweat, toil and bleed, face the abyss. It's all part of becoming an overnight success.

If you had to pass down to your kids one or two principles, what would they be?

Number one: read. Read everything you can. And not just the stuff that society tells you is good or even books that I tell you to read. Just read for its own sake. Develop a love for it. Even if you have to read romance novels or paperbacks or comic books. There's no such thing as junk. Just read it all. Eventually, you'll guide yourself to the things that you should and want to be reading.

Related to the skill of reading are the skills of mathematics and persuasion. Both skills help you to navigate through the real world.

Having the skill of persuasion is important because if you can influence your fellow human beings, you can get a lot done. I think persuasion is an actual skill. So you can learn it, and it's not that hard to do so.

Mathematics helps with all the complex and difficult things in life. If you want to make money, if you want to do science, if you want to understand game theory or politics or economics or investments or computers, all of these things have mathematics at the core. It's a foundational language of nature.

Nature speaks in mathematics. Mathematics is us reverse engineering the language of nature, and we have only scratched the surface. The good news is you don't have to know a lot of math. You just have to know basic statistics, arithmetic, etc. You should know statistics and probability forwards and backwards and inside out.

CHOOSING TO FREE YOURSELF

> The hardest thing is not doing what you want—it's knowing what you want.

Be aware there are no "adults." Everyone makes it up as they go along. You have to find your own path, picking, choosing, and discarding as you see fit. Figure it out yourself, and do it.

How have your values changed?

When I was younger, I really, really valued freedom. Freedom was one of my core values. Ironically, it still is. It's probably one of my top three values, but it's now a different definition of freedom.

My old definition was "freedom to." Freedom to do anything I want. Freedom to do whatever I feel like, whenever I feel like. Now, the freedom I'm looking for is internal freedom. It's "freedom from." Freedom from reaction. Freedom from feeling angry. Freedom from being sad. Freedom from being forced to do things. I'm looking for "freedom from," internally and externally, whereas before I was looking for "freedom to."

> Advice to my younger self: "Be exactly who you are."
>
> Holding back means staying in bad relationships and bad jobs for years instead of minutes.

FREEDOM FROM EXPECTATIONS

I don't measure my effectiveness at all. I don't believe in self-measurement. I feel like this is a form of self-discipline, self-punishment, and self-conflict.

If you hurt other people because they have expectations of you, that's their problem. If they have an agreement with you, it's your problem. But, if they have an expectation of you, that's completely their problem. It has nothing to do with you. They're going to have lots of expectations out of life. The sooner you can dash their expectations, the better.

> Courage isn't charging into a machine gun nest. Courage is not caring what other people think.

Anyone who has known me for a long time knows my defining characteristic is a combination of being very impatient and willful. I don't like to wait. I hate wasting time. I'm very famous for being rude at parties, events, dinners, where the moment I figure out it's a waste of my time, I leave immediately.

Value your time. It is all you have. It's more important than your money. It's more important than your friends. It is more important than anything. Your time is all you have. Do not waste your time.

This doesn't mean you can't relax. As long as you're doing what you want, it's not a waste of your time. But if you're not spending your time doing what you want, and you're not earning, and you're not learning—what the heck are you doing?

Don't spend your time making other people happy. Other people being happy is their problem. It's not your problem. If you are happy, it makes other people happy. If you're happy, other people will ask you how you became happy and they might learn from it, but you are not responsible for making other people happy.

FREEDOM FROM ANGER

What is anger? Anger is a way to signal as strongly as you can to the other party you're capable of violence. Anger is a precursor to violence.

Observe when you're angry—anger is a loss of control over the situation. Anger is a contract you make with yourself to be in physical and mental and emotional turmoil until reality changes.

> Anger is its own punishment. An angry person trying to push your head below water is drowning at the same time.

FREEDOM FROM EMPLOYMENT

People who live far below their means enjoy a freedom that people busy upgrading their lifestyles can't fathom.

Once you've truly controlled your own fate, for better or for worse, you'll never let anyone else tell you what to do.

> A taste of freedom can make you unemployable.

FREEDOM FROM UNCONTROLLED THINKING

A big habit I'm working on is trying to turn off my "monkey mind." When we're children, we're pretty blank slates. We live very much in the moment. We essentially just react to our environment through our instincts. We live in what I would call the "real world." Puberty is the onset of desire—the first time you really, really want something and you start long-range planning. You start thinking a lot, building an identity and an ego to get what you want.

If you walk down the street and there are a thousand people in the street, all thousand are talking to themselves in their head at any given point. They're constantly judging everything they see. They're playing back movies of things that happened to them yesterday. They're living in fantasy worlds of what's going to happen tomorrow. They're just pulled out of base reality. That can be good when you do long-range planning. It can be good when you solve problems. It's good for us as survival-and-replication machines.

I think it's actually very bad for your happiness. To me, the mind should be a servant and a tool, not a master. My monkey mind should not control and drive me 24/7.

I want to break the habit of uncontrolled thinking, which is hard.

> A busy mind accelerates the passage of subjective time.

There is no endpoint to self-awareness and self-discovery. It's a lifelong process you hopefully keep getting better and better at. There is no one meaningful answer, and no one is going to fully solve it unless you're one of these enlightened characters. Maybe some of us will get there, but I'm not likely to, given how involved I am in the rat race. The best case is I'm a rat who might be able to look up at the clouds once in a while.

I think just being aware you're a rat in a race is about as far as most of us are going to get.

> The modern struggle:
>
> Lone individuals summoning inhuman willpower, fasting, meditating, and exercising…
>
> Up against armies of scientists and statisticians weaponizing abundant food, screens, and medicine into junk food, clickbait news, infinite porn, endless games, and addictive drugs.

I PHILOSOPHY

> The real truths are heresies. They cannot be spoken. Only discovered, whispered, and perhaps read.

THE MEANINGS OF LIFE

A really unbounded, big question: what is the meaning and purpose of life?

That's a big question. Because it's a big question, I'll give you three answers.

Answer 1: It's personal. You have to find your own meaning. Any piece of wisdom anybody else gives you, whether it's Buddha or me, is going to sound like nonsense. Fundamentally, you have to find it for yourself, so the important part is not the answer, it's the question. You just have to sit there and dig with the question. It might take you years or decades. When you find an answer you're happy with, it will be fundamental to your life.

Answer 2: There is no meaning to life. There is no purpose to life. Osho said, "It's like writing on water or building houses of sand." The reality is you've been dead for the history of the Universe, 10 billion years or more. You will be dead for the next 70 billion years or so, until the heat death of the Universe.

Anything you do will fade. It will disappear, just like the human race will disappear and the planet will disappear. Even the group who colonizes Mars will disappear. No one is going to remember you past a certain number of generations, whether you're an artist, a poet, a conqueror, a pauper, or anyone else. There's no meaning.

You have to create your own meaning, which is what it boils down to. You have to decide:

"Is this a play I'm just watching?"

"Is there a self-actualization dance I'm doing?"

"Is there a specific thing I desire just for the heck of it?"

These are all meanings you make up.

There is no fundamental, intrinsic purposeful meaning to the Universe. If there was, then you would just ask the next question. You'd say, "Why is that the meaning?" It would be, as physicist Richard Feynman said, it would be "turtles all the way down." The "why's" would keep accumulating. There is no answer you could give that wouldn't have another "why."

I don't buy the everlasting afterlife answers because it's insane to me, with absolutely no evidence, to believe because of how you live seventy years here on this planet, you're going to spend eternity, which is a very long time, in some afterlife. What kind of silly God judges you for eternity based on some small period of time here? I think after this life, it's very much like before you were born. Remember that? It's going to be just like that.

Before you were born, you didn't care about anything or anyone, including your loved ones, including yourself, including humans, including whether we go to Mars or whether we stay on planet Earth, whether there's an AI or not. After death, you just don't care either.

Answer 3: The last answer I'll give you is a little more complicated. From what I've read in science (friends of mine have written books on this), I've stitched together some theories. Maybe there is a meaning to life, but it's not a very satisfying purpose.

Basically, in physics, the arrow of time comes from entropy.

The second law of thermodynamics states entropy only goes up, which means disorder in the Universe only goes up, which means concentrated free energy only goes down. If you look at living things (humans, plants, civilizations, what have you) these systems are locally reversing entropy. Humans locally reverse entropy because we have action.

In the process, we globally accelerate entropy until the heat death of the Universe. You could come up with some fanciful theory, which I like, that we're headed towards the heat death of the Universe. In that death, there's no concentrated energy, and everything is at the same energy level. Therefore, we're all one thing. We're essentially indistinguishable.

What we do as living systems accelerates getting to that state. The more complex system you create, whether it's through computers, civilization, art, mathematics, or creating a family—you actually accelerate the heat death of the Universe. You're pushing us towards this point where we end up as one thing.

LIVE BY YOUR VALUES

What are your core values?

I've never fully enumerated them, but a few examples:

Honesty is a core, core, core value. By honesty, I mean I want to be able to just be me. I never want to be in an environment or around people where I have to watch what I say. If I disconnect what I'm thinking from what I'm saying, it creates multiple threads in my mind. I'm no longer in the moment—now I have to be future-planning or past-regretting every time I talk to somebody. Anyone around whom I can't be fully honest, I don't want to be around.

> Before you can lie to another, you must first lie to yourself.

Another example of a foundational value: I don't believe in any short-term thinking or dealing. If I'm doing business with somebody and they think in a short-term manner with somebody else, then I don't want to do business with them anymore. All benefits in life come from compound interest, whether in money, relationships, love, health, activities, or habits. I only want to be around people I know I'm going to be around for the rest of my life. I only want to work on things I know have long-term payout.

Another one is I only believe in peer relationships. I don't believe in hierarchical relationships. I don't want to be above anybody, and I don't want to be below anybody. If I can't treat someone like a peer and if they can't treat me like peer, I just don't want to interact with them.

Another: I don't believe in anger anymore. Anger was good when I was young and full of testosterone, but now I like the Buddhist saying, "Anger is a hot coal you hold in your hand while waiting to throw it at somebody." I don't want to be angry, and I don't want to be around angry people. I just cut them out of my life. I'm not judging them. I went through a lot of anger too. They have to work through it on their own. Go be angry at someone else, somewhere else.

I don't know if these necessarily fall into the classical definition of values, but it's a set of things I won't compromise on and I live my entire life by. I think everybody has values. Much of finding great relationships, great coworkers, great lovers, wives, husbands, is finding other people where your values line up. If your values line up, the little things don't matter. Generally, I find if people are fighting or quarreling about something, it's because their values don't line up. If their values lined up, the little things wouldn't matter.

Meeting my wife was a great test because I really wanted to be with her, and she wasn't so sure at the beginning. In the end, we ended up together because she saw my values. I am lucky I had developed them by that point. If I hadn't, I wouldn't have gotten her. I wouldn't have deserved her. As investor Charlie Munger says, "To find a worthy mate, be worthy of a worthy mate."

My wife is an incredibly lovely, family-oriented person, and so am I. That was one of the foundational values that brought us together.

The moment you have a child, it's this really weird thing, but it answers the meaning-of-life, purpose-of-life, question. All of a sudden, the most important thing in the Universe moves from being in your body into the child's body. That changes you. Your values inherently become a lot less selfish.

RATIONAL BUDDHISM

> The older the question, the older the answers.

You've called your philosophy Rational Buddhism. How does it differ from traditional Buddhism? What type of exploration did you go through?

The rational part means I have to reconcile with science and evolution. I have to reject all the pieces I can't verify for myself. For example, is meditation good for you? Yes. Is clearing your mind a good thing? Yes. Is there a base layer of awareness below your monkey mind? Yes. All these things I've verified for myself.

Some beliefs from Buddhism I believe and follow because, again, I've verified or reasoned with thought experiments myself. What I will not accept is things like, "There's a past life you're paying off the karma for." I haven't seen it. I don't remember any past lives. I don't have any memory. I just have to not believe that.

When people say your third chakra is opening, etc.—I don't know—that's just fancy nomenclature. I have not been able to verify or confirm any of that on my own. If I can't verify it on my own or if I cannot get there through science, then it may be true, it may be false, but it's not falsifiable, so I cannot view it as a fundamental truth.

On the other side, I do know evolution is true. I do know we are evolved as survival and replication machines. I do know we have an ego, so we get up off the ground and worms don't eat us and we actually take action. Rational Buddhism, to me, means understanding the internal work Buddhism espouses to make yourself happier, better off, more present and in control of your emotions—being a better human being.

I don't subscribe to anything fanciful because it was written down in a book. I don't think I can levitate. I don't think meditation will give me superpowers and those kinds of things. Try everything, test it for yourself, be skeptical, keep what's useful, and discard what's not.

I would say my philosophy falls down to this—on one pole is evolution as a binding principle because it explains so much about humans, on the other is Buddhism, which is the oldest, most time-tested spiritual philosophy regarding the internal state of each of us.

I think those are absolutely reconcilable. I actually want to write a blog post at some point about how you can map the tenets of Buddhism, especially the non-fanciful ones, directly into a virtual reality simulation.

> Everyone starts out innocent. Everyone is corrupted. Wisdom is the discarding of vices and the return to virtue, by way of knowledge.

How do you define wisdom?

Understanding the long-term consequences of your actions.

> If wisdom could be imparted through words alone, we'd all be done here.

THE PRESENT IS ALL WE HAVE

There is actually nothing but this moment. No one has ever gone back in time, and no one has ever been able to successfully predict the future in any way that matters. Literally, the only thing that exists is this exact point where you are in space at the exact time you happen to be here.

Like all great profound truths, it's all paradoxes. Any two points are infinitely different. Any moment is perfectly unique. Each moment itself slips by so quickly you can't grab it.

You're dying and being reborn at every moment. It's up to you whether to forget or remember that.

> "Everything is more beautiful because we're doomed. You will never be lovelier than you are now, and we will never be here again."
>
> —Homer, The Iliad

I don't even remember what I said two minutes ago. At best, the past is some fictional little memory tape in my head. As far as I'm concerned, my past is dead. It's gone. All death really means is that there are no more future moments.

> Inspiration is perishable—act on it immediately.

INSPIRATION IS PERISHABLE, ACT ON IT IMMEDIATELY.

BONUS

> The democratization of technology allows anyone to be a creator, entrepreneur, scientist. The future is brighter.

It's statistically likely there are more advanced alien civilizations out there.

Hopefully, they're good environmentalists and find us cute.

NAVAL'S RECOMMENDED READING

> The truth is, I don't read for self-improvement. I read out of curiosity and interest. The best book is the one you'll devour.

BOOKS

(Since there are so many links in this section, you may prefer a digital copy. Go to Navalmanack.com to get a digital version of this chapter for your convenience.)

> Read enough, and you become a connoisseur. Then you naturally gravitate more toward theory, concepts, nonfiction.

NONFICTION

The Beginning of Infinity: Explanations That Transform the World by David Deutsch

Not the easiest read, but it made me smarter.

Sapiens: A Brief History of Humankind by Yuval Noah Harari

A history of the human species. The observations, frameworks, and mental models will have you looking at history and your fellow humans differently.

Sapiens is the best book of the last decade I have read. He had decades to write *Sapiens*. There are lots of great ideas in there and it's just full of them, chock-full per page.

The Rational Optimist: How Prosperity Evolves by Matt Ridley

The most brilliant and enlightening book I've read in years. He has written four of my top twenty books.

Everything else written by Matt Ridley. Matt is a scientist, optimist, and forward thinker. One of my favorite authors. I've read everything of his, and reread everything of his.

- → Genome: The Autobiography of a Species in 23 Chapters
- → The Red Queen: Sex and the Evolution of Human Nature
- → The Origins of Virtue: Human Instincts and the Evolution of Cooperation
- → The Evolution of Everything: How New Ideas Emerge

Skin in the Game by Nassim Taleb

The best book I read in 2018, I highly recommend it. Lots of great ideas in there. Lots of good mental models and constructs. He has a bit of an attitude, but he has that because he's brilliant, and it's okay. So just look past the attitude and read the book, learn the concepts. It's one of the best business books I've ever read. And luckily, it doesn't masquerade as a business book.

The Bed of Procrustes: Philosophical and Practical Aphorisms by Nassim Taleb

This is his collection of ancient wisdom. He is also famous for *The Black Swan: The Impact of the Highly Improbable, Antifragile: Things That Gain from Disorder,* and *Fooled by Randomness: The Hidden Role of Chance in Life and in the Markets,* all of which are worth reading.

Six Easy Pieces: Essentials of Physics Explained by Its Most Brilliant Teacher by Richard Feynman

I would give my kids a copy of Richard Feynman's *Six Easy Pieces* and *Six Not-So-Easy Pieces: Einstein's Relativity, Symme-*

try, and Space-Time. Richard Feynman is a famous physicist. I love both his demeanor as well as his understanding of physics.

I've also been reading *Perfectly Reasonable Deviations from the Beaten Track* by Feynman and rereading *Genius: The Life and Science of Richard Feynman*, a biography about him.

Thing Explainer: Complicated Stuff in Simple Words by Randall Munroe

A great book by Randall Munroe (creator of *xkcd*, a very science-oriented webcomic). In this book, he explains very complicated concepts, all the way from climate change to physical systems to submarines while only using the thousand most common words in the English language. He called the Saturn Five rocket "Up Goer Five." You can't define a rocket as a spaceship or a rocket. It's self-referential. He says "up goer." It's this thing that goes up. Kids get it right away.

Thinking Physics: Understandable Practical Reality by Lewis Carroll Epstein

There's another great book called *Thinking Physics*. I open this one all the time. I love on the back cover how it has this great little pitch that says, "The only book used in both grade school and graduate school." It's true. It's all simple physics puzzles that can be explained to a twelve-year-old child and can be explained to a twenty-five-year-old grad student in physics. They all have fundamental insights in physics. They're all kind of tricky, but anyone can get to the answer through purely logical reasoning.

The Lessons of History by Will and Ariel Durant

This is a great book I really like that summarizes some of the larger themes of history; it's very incisive. And unlike most history books, it's actually really small, and it covers a lot of ground.

The Sovereign Individual: Mastering the Transition to the Information Age by James Dale Davidson and Lord William Rees-Mogg

This is the best book I've read since *Sapiens* (far less mainstream, though).

Poor Charlie's Almanack: The Wit and Wisdom of Charles T. Munger by Charlie Munger (edited by Peter Kaufman)

This masquerades as a business book, but it's really just Charlie Munger (of Berkshire Hathaway)'s advice on overcoming oneself to live a successful and virtuous life.

Reality Is Not What It Seems: The Journey to Quantum Gravity by Carlo Rovelli

This is the best book I've read in the last year. Physics, poetry, philosophy, and history packaged in a very accessible form.

Seven Brief Lessons on Physics by Carlo Rovelli

I've read this one at least twice.

For game theory, in addition to playing strategy games, you may want to try *The Compleat Strategyst: Being a Primer on the Theory of Games of Strategy* by J.D. Williams and *The Evolution of Cooperation* by Robert Axelrod.

PHILOSOPHY AND SPIRITUALITY

Everything by Jed McKenna

Jed spits raw truth. His style may be off-putting, but the dedication to truth is unparalleled.

Theory of Everything (The Enlightened Perspective) - Dreamstate Trilogy

Jed McKenna's Notebook

Jed Talks #1 and #2

Everything by Kapil Gupta, MD

Kapil recently became a personal advisor and coach to me, and this comes from a person who doesn't believe in coaches.

A Master's Secret Whispers: For those who abhor noise and seek The Truth...about life and living

Direct Truth: Uncompromising, non-prescriptive Truths to the enduring questions of life

Atmamun: The Path to achieving the bliss of the Himalayan Swamis. And the freedom of a living God.

The Book of Life by Jiddu Krishnamurti

Krishnamurti is a lesser-known guy, an Indian philosopher who lived at the turn of the last century and is extremely influential to me. He's an uncompromising, very direct person who basically tells you to look at your own mind at all times. I have been hugely influenced by him. Probably the best book is *The Book of Life*, which is excerpts from his various speeches and books stitched together.

I'll give my kids a copy of *The Book of Life*. I'll tell them to save it until they're older because it won't make much sense while they're younger.

Total Freedom: The Essential Krishnamurti by Jiddu Krishnamurti

I like this for someone who's more advanced. A rationalist's guide to the perils of the human mind. The "spiritual" book I keep returning to.

Siddhartha by Herman Hesse

I love this as a classic book on philosophy, a good introduction for someone starting out. I've given out more copies of this book than any other.

> I'm pretty much always rereading something by either Krishnamurti or Osho. Those are my favorite philosophers.

[Update: I'd now add Jed McKenna, Kapil Gupta, the Vashistha Yoga, and Schopenhauer to that list.]

The Book of Secrets: 112 Meditations to Discover the Mystery Within by Osho

Most meditation techniques are concentration methods, and

there are many, many meditation techniques. If you want to run through a bunch of them, you can pick up a book called *The Book of Secrets* by Osho. I know he's gotten a bad rap recently, but he was a pretty smart guy. It's actually a translation of an old Sanskrit book with 112 different meditations. You can try each one and see which one works for you.

The Great Challenge: Exploring the World Within by Osho

The Way to Love: The Last Meditations of Anthony de Mello by Anthony de Mello

The Untethered Soul: The Journey Beyond Yourself by Michael Singer

Meditations by Marcus Aurelius

Marcus Aurelius was absolutely life-changing for me. It's the personal diary of the emperor of Rome. Here's a guy who was probably the most powerful human being on Earth at the time he lived. He's writing a diary to himself, never expecting it to be published. When you open this book, you realize he had all the same issues and all the same mental struggles; he was trying to be a better person. Right there, you figure out success and power don't improve your internal state—you still have to work on it.

Love Yourself Like Your Life Depends on It by Kamal Ravikant

I've actually been reading my brother's book, *Love Yourself Like Your Life Depends on It*. I thought it was very succinctly written. (Obviously a plug for my bro.)

He's the philosopher in the family—I'm just the amateur. He has a great line in his book:

> I once asked a monk how he found peace.
>
> "I say 'yes,'" he'd said. "To all that happens, I say 'yes.'"

The Tao of Seneca: Practical Letters from a Stoic Master

My most listened-to audiobook. The most important audiobook I've ever heard.

How to Change Your Mind by Michael Pollan

There's a good book Michael Pollan wrote recently called *How to Change Your Mind*, and I think it is a brilliant book everybody should read.

The book discusses psychedelics. Psychedelics are a bit of a cheat code in self-observation. I don't recommend drugs for anybody—you can do it all through pure meditation. If you want to accelerate ahead, you know, psychedelics are good for that.

Striking Thoughts: Bruce Lee's Wisdom for Daily Living by Bruce Lee

Oddly enough, Bruce Lee wrote some great philosophy, and *Striking Thoughts* is a good summary of some of his philosophy.

The Prophet by Kahlil Gibran

This book reads like a modern-day poetic religious tome. It's up there with the Bhagavad Gita, the *Tao Te Ching*, the Bible, and the Qur'an. It is written in the style where it has a feel of religiosity and truth, but it was very approachable, beautiful, nondenominational, and nonsectarian. I loved this book.

He has a gift for poetically describing what children are like, what lovers are like, what marriage should be like, how you should treat your enemies and your friends, how you should work with money, what can you think of every time you have to kill something to eat it. I felt it, like the great religious books, gave a very deep, very philosophical, but very true answer to how to approach the major problems in life. I recommend *The Prophet* to anybody, whether you're religious or not. Whether you are Christian, Hindu, Jewish, or atheist. I think it's a beautiful book, and it's worth reading.

SCIENCE FICTION

> I started with comic books and sci-fi. Then I was into history and news. Then into psychology, popular science, technology.

Ficciones by Jorge Luis Borges

I love Jorge Luis Borges, an Argentine author. His short story collection *Ficciones*, or *Labyrinths*, is amazing. Borges is probably still the most powerful author I have read who wasn't just outright writing philosophy. There was philosophy in there with the sci-fi.

Stories of Your Life and Others by Ted Chiang

My current favorite sci-fi short story: probably "Understand" by Ted Chiang. It's in a collection called *Stories of Your Life and Others*. "Story of Your Life" was made into a movie called *Arrival*.

Exhalation: Stories by Ted Chiang

This contemplates the marvel of thermodynamics from the best sci-fi short story writer of our age.

The Lifecycle of Software Objects by Ted Chiang

Another masterpiece of sci-fi by Ted Chiang.

Snow Crash by Neal Stephenson

Snow Crash is an amazing, amazing book. There's nothing quite similar to *Snow Crash*. *Snow Crash* is in a league of its own. Stephenson also wrote *The Diamond Age*.

"The Last Question," a short story by Isaac Asimov

I quote "The Last Question" all the time. I loved it as a kid.

What are the books you're rereading now?

That's a good question. I'll pull up my Kindle app as we talk. Usually, I'm always rereading some books in science.

I'm reading a book on René Girard's mimetic theory. It's more of an overview book, because I couldn't make it through his actual writings. I'm reading *Tools of Titans*, Tim Ferriss's book of what he learned from a lot of great performers.

I'm reading a book, *Thermoinfocomplexity*. It's actually by a friend of mine, Behzad Mohit. I just finished reading *Pre-Suasion: A Revolutionary Way to Influence and Persuade*, or I should say I just finished skimming *Pre-Suasion* by Robert Cialdini. I don't think I needed to read the entire book to get the point, but it was still good to read what I did. It's a great little history book. I'm currently reading *The Story of Philosophy: The Lives and Opinions of the Great Philosophers*, also by Will Durant.

I have a young kid now, so I've got a lot of child-rearing books I use more as reference material than anything else. I recently read some Emerson and some Chesterfield. I have a Leo Tolstoy book here.

Alan Watts. Scott Adams. I reread *God's Debris* recently. *Tao Te Ching*, a friend of mine is rereading it, so I picked it up again. There's tons. I mean, I could go on and on. There's Nietzsche's book here. There's *The Undercover Economist* [Tim Harford]. The Richard Bach book [*Illusions: The Adventures of a Reluctant Messiah*]. There are some Jed McKenna books.

A little Dale Carnegie in here. *The Three-Body Problem* [Cixin Liu]. *Man's Search for Meaning* [Viktor E. Frankl]. There's lots. *Sex at Dawn* [Christopher Ryan]. There's a lot of books out there.

By the way, when I tell people what I'm reading, I skip two-thirds of my books. The reason I skip two-thirds is because they're embarrassing. They don't sound like good books to read. They'll sound trivial or silly. Who cares? I don't have to tell everybody everything I read. I read all kinds of stuff other people consider junk or even reprehensible. I read all kinds of stuff I disagree with because they're mind-bending.

> I always spent money on books. I never viewed that as an expense. That's an investment to me.

BLOGS

(Since there are so many links in this section, you may prefer a digital copy. Go to Navalmanack.com to get a digital version of this chapter for your convenience.)

Some amazing blogs out there:

@KevinSimler—*Melting Asphalt*, https://meltingasphalt.com/

@farnamstreet—*Farnam Street, A Signal in a World Full of Noise*, https://fs.blog/

@benthompson—*Stratchery*, https://stratechery.com/

@baconmeteor—*Idle Words*, https://idlewords.com/

"The Munger Operating System: How to Live a Life That Really Works" by @FarnamStreet

Rules to live and prosper by.

"The Day You Became a Better Writer" by Scott Adams

Even though I am a very good writer and I've been writing a lot since I was young, I still open up that blog post and put it in the background anytime I'm writing anything important. It's that good. I use it as my basic template for how to write well. Think about the title, "The Day You Became a Better Writer." It's such a powerful title. He teaches you in one small blog post the importance of surprise, the importance of headlines, the importance of being brief and directed, not using some adjectives and adverbs, using active not the passive voice, etc. This one blog post right there will change your writing style forever if you put your ego down and absorb it properly.

Want to become smarter in ten minutes? Absorb this: "Crony Beliefs" by Kevin Simler.

Best post I've read on "Career Decisions" (in Silicon Valley/tech) by @eladgil

Harari's *Sapiens* in lecture/course form on YouTube.

Every business school should have a course on Aggregation Theory. Or learn it from the master himself, @benthompson, the best analyst in technology.

Great read. "Quantum physics is not 'weird.' *You* are weird."—"Think Like Reality" [Eliezer Yudkowsky]

Must-read. "Lazy Leadership" by @Awilkinson

No-holds-barred wisdom from a self-made man. Everything on @EdLatimore's site is worth reading for overachievers: https://edlatimore.com/

> If you eat, invest, and think according to what the "news" advocates, you'll end up nutritionally, financially, and morally bankrupt.

OTHER RECOMMENDATIONS

Twitter accounts like:

@AmuseChimp (my all-time favorite Twitter account)

@mmay3r

@nntaleb

Art De Vany (on Facebook)

Genius is here, just unevenly distributed.

Must-read. (Twitter thread on "intellectual compounding" by @zaoyang).

There are actually some really good graphic novels out there. If you're open to the cartoony element of it, *Transmetropolitan* [Warren Ellis], *The Boys* [Garth Ennis], *Planetary* [Warren Ellis], and *The Sandman* [Neil Gaiman]...some of these are, I think, among the finest works of art of our age. I also grew up as a boy reading comics, so I may be very biased toward those.

Rick and Morty (TV show + comic book)

Rick and Morty is the best show on television (IMHO, of course).

Just watch the first episode—that's all it takes. It's *Back to the Future* meets *The Hitchhiker's Guide to the Galaxy*.

The *Rick and Morty* comic [by Zac Gorman] is just as clever as the show.

"You and Your Research" by Richard Hamming

A beautiful essay, I highly recommend reading it. It's ostensibly written for people who are in scientific research, but I think it applies across the board. It's just an old-timer essay on how to do great work. It reminds me of much of what Richard Feynman used to say, although I think Hamming has put it more eloquently than almost anywhere else I've seen.

I NAVAL'S WRITING

LIFE FORMULAS I (2008)

These are notes to myself. Your frame of reference, and therefore your calculations, may vary. These are not definitions—these are algorithms for success. Contributions are welcome.

- → Happiness = Health + Wealth + Good Relationships
- → Health = Exercise + Diet + Sleep
- → Exercise = High Intensity Resistance Training + Sports + Rest
- → Diet = Natural Foods + Intermittent Fasting + Plants
- → Sleep = No alarms + 8–9 hours + Circadian rhythms
- → Wealth = Income + Wealth * (Return on Investment)
- → Income = Accountability + Leverage + Specific Knowledge
- → Accountability = Personal Branding + Personal Platform + Taking Risk?
- → Leverage = Capital + People + Intellectual Property
- → Specific Knowledge = Knowing how to do something society cannot yet easily train other people to do
- → Return on Investment = "Buy-and-Hold" + Valuation + Margin of Safety

NAVAL'S RULES (2016)

- → Be present above all else.
- → Desire is suffering. (Buddha)
- → Anger is a hot coal you hold in your hand while waiting to throw it at someone else. (Buddha)
- → If you can't see yourself working with someone for life, don't work with them for a day.
- → Reading (learning) is the ultimate meta-skill and can be traded for anything else.
- → All the real benefits in life come from compound interest.
- → Earn with your mind, not your time.
- → 99 percent of all effort is wasted.
- → Total honesty at all times. It's almost always possible to be honest and positive.
- → Praise specifically, criticize generally. (Warren Buffett)
- → Truth is that which has predictive power.
- → Watch every thought. (Ask "Why am I having this thought?")
- → All greatness comes from suffering.
- → Love is given, not received.
- → Enlightenment is the space between your thoughts. (Eckhart Tolle)
- → Mathematics is the language of nature.
- → Every moment has to be complete in and of itself.

> Health, love, and your mission, in that order. Nothing else matters.

I NEXT ON NAVAL

If you loved this book, there are many ways to dive deeper into Naval. I am publishing "Navalmanack" shorts on Navalmanack.com. These are sections that were edited out of the original (enormous) manuscript of this book. I've published them online for those interested in Naval's more specific insights on:

→ Education
→ The Story of AngelList
→ Investing
→ Startups
→ Crypto
→ Relationships

Naval continues to create and share great insights:

→ On Twitter: Twitter.com/Naval
→ On his podcast: *Naval*
→ On his website: https://nav.al/

The most popular of Naval's material at the time of writing:

→ *Naval* podcast episodes compilation:How to Get Rich

- → Interview on The Knowledge Project
- → Interview on Joe Rogan Podcast

Readwise.io has generously created a collection of excerpts of this book, available through Readwise.io/naval. You will receive a weekly email with key excerpts from this book to keep the concepts top-of-mind long after you've finished reading.

If you love the illustrations by Jack Butcher, you can find more of his illustrations of Naval's ideas on Navalmanack.com and more of his work at VisualizeValue.com.

I APPRECIATION

There is so much to be grateful for, and so many people to be grateful to. I am overwhelmed with happiness when I consider all of the people who contributed pieces of themselves to create this book. I feel a rising, inflating warmth of gratitude for all of you.

Here is my written Oscars speech of thanks and appreciation:

I'm extremely grateful to Naval for trusting a stranger from the internet to create a book out of his words. This all started with a half-assed tweet, and became something great because of your trust and support. I appreciate your responsiveness, generosity, and trust.

I am grateful to Babak Nivi for the most succinct and precise writing advice I've ever received. You have been generous with your time to make this book better, and I really appreciate it.

I am grateful to Tim Ferriss for bending your iron rule and writing the foreword for this book. Your presence in this project means a lot to me and will certainly help many more people find their way to Naval's wisdom.

The building blocks of this book are excerpts from excellent interviews of creators like Shane Parrish, Joe Rogan, Sarah Lacy, and Tim Ferriss. I massively appreciate all of the effort that goes into your interviews. Creating this book gave me and others the opportunity to learn deeply from your work.

I am grateful to Jack Butcher for reaching out and offering to lend his enormous talents to creating the illustrations for this book. His work at Visualize Value has always struck me as simple genius, and we're all lucky to have his efforts in these pages.

I am grateful to my parents for every gift, effort, and sacrifice that has put me in a position to create this book. You built the foundation of everything I ever do, and I'll never forget that. The family practice of "spitting your doubts" is alive and well in this project.

I am grateful to Jeannine Seidl for being a one-woman support system of love and encouragement. You are an endless spring of positivity, patience, and good advice. Thank you for always keeping morale high.

I am grateful to Kathleen Martin for being a truly wonderful line editor and doing her very best work on this project. (And thanks to David Perell for introducing us.)

I am grateful to Kusal Kularatne for his many contributions. You were an early believer, an early reader, and a huge help when this project was young and fragile. I appreciate you and thank you for your service.

I am grateful to Max Olson, Emily Holdman, and Taylor Pearson. You are all wonderful friends who became extremely helpful advisors to me throughout this book-building and publishing process. Without you, I'd still be googling things and mumbling curses.

I am grateful to my posse of early readers for their time, edits, and wise advice. Every one of you made valuable contributions to this book, and it wouldn't be what it is without you. My deepest appreciation for each of you: Andrew Farah, Tristan Homsi, Daniel Doyon, Jessie Jacobs, Sean O'Connor, Adam Waxman, Kaylan Perry, Chris Quintero, George Mack, Brent Beshore, Shane Parrish, Taylor Pearson, Ben Crane, Candace Wu, Shane Mac, Jesse Powers, Trevor McKendrick, David Perell, Natala Constantine, Ben Jackson, Noah Madden, Chris Gillett, Megan Darnell, and Zach Anderson Pettet.

I am grateful to the authors and creators who inspired this book. My drive to create and share this book came directly out of a deep appreciation for the life-changing impact of similar books, a few I'd like to name specifically:

- → *Poor Charlie's Almanack* edited by Peter Kaufman (of Charlie Munger's work)
- → *Zero to One* by Blake Masters (of Peter Thiel's work)
- → *Seeking Wisdom* (and others) by Peter Bevelin (of Buffett and Munger's work)
- → *Berkshire Hathaway Letters to Shareholders* edited by Max Olson (of Buffett's work)
- → *Principles* by Ray Dalio (and team)

I am grateful to the team at Scribe, for being early and earnest supporters of this book. Zach Obront provides fantastic advice, and Hal Clifford is a patient and persistent editor.

I am grateful to Tucker Max for creating Scribe, hiring a great team, and for the very personal attention and effort in this project. I appreciate your willingness to hurt my feelings in pursuit of a great product. And I deeply appreciate your trust in me to do good work.

I am grateful to Bo and the whole team at Zaarly for their patience and grace around my obsession with this book and the effort that went into it.

I am grateful for the support of many friends and strangers online who supported and encouraged me throughout this project. My DMs overflow with kind words and eager inquiries. I appreciate every gesture. Your energy helped pull me through the thousand hours it took to create this for you.

I SOURCES

Line-by-line citations have been removed from this version. A fully cited version of this book is available at Navalmanack.com.

[1] Ravikant, Naval. "Naval Ravikant Was Live." *Periscope*, January 20, 2018. https://www.pscp.tv/w/1eaKbqrWloRxX.

[2] Ravikant, Naval. "Naval Ravikant Was Live." *Periscope*, February 11, 2018. https://www.pscp.tv/w/1MnGneBLZVmKO.

[3] Ferriss, Tim. *Tribe of Mentors: Short Life Advice from the Best in the World.* New York: Houghton Mifflin Harcourt, 2017. https://amzn.to/2U2kE3b.

[4] Ravikant, Naval and Shane Parrish. "Naval Ravikant: The Angel Philosopher." *Farnam Street*, 2019. https://fs.blog/naval-ravikant/.

[5] Ferriss, Tim. *Tools of Titans: The Tactics, Routines, and Habits of Billionaires, Icons, and World-Class Performers.* New York: Houghton Mifflin Harcourt, 2016.

[6] Ferriss, Tim. "The Person I Call Most Often for Startup Advice (#97)." *The Tim Ferriss Show*, August 18, 2015. https://tim.blog/2015/08/18/the-evolutionary-angel-naval-ravikant/.

[7] Ferriss, Tim. "Naval Ravikant on the Tim Ferriss Show—Transcript." *The Tim Ferriss Show*, 2019. https://tim.blog/naval-ravikant-on-the-tim-ferriss-show-transcript/.

[8] *Killing Buddha* Interviews. "Chief Executive Philosopher: Naval Ravikant On Suffering and Acceptance." *Killing Buddha*, 2016. http://www.killingbuddha.co/blog/2016/2/7/naval-ravikant-ceo-of-angellist; "Chief Executive Philosopher: Naval Ravikant On the Skill of Happiness." *Killing Buddha*, 2016. http://www.killingbuddha.co/blog/2016/2/10/chief-executive-philosopher-naval-on-happiness-as-peace-and-choosing-your-desires-carefully; "Chief Executive Philosopher: Naval Ravikant On Who He Admires." *Killing Buddha*, 2016. http://www.killingbuddha.co/blog/2016/2/19/naval-ravikant-on-who-he-admires; "Chief Executive Philosopher: Naval Ravikant On the Give and Take of the Modern World." *Killing Buddha*, 2016. http://www.killingbuddha.co/blog/2016/2/23/old-bodies-in-a-new-world; "Chief Executive Philosopher: Naval Ravikant On Travelling Lightly." *Killing Buddha*, 2016. http://www.killingbuddha.co/blog/2016/9/19/naval-ravikant-on-travelling-lightly; "Naval Ravikant on Wim Hof, His Advice to His Children, and How He Wants to Look Back on His Life." *Killing Buddha*, 2016. http://www.killingbuddha.co/blog/2016/12/28/naval-ravikant-on-advice-to-his-children.

[9] DeSena, Joe. "155: It's All About Your Desires, Says AngelList Founder Naval Ravikant." *Spartan Up!*, 2019. https://player.fm/series/spartan-up-audio/155-its-all-about-your-desires-says-angel-list-founder-naval-ravikantunder-naval-ravikant.

[10] "Naval Ravikant was live." *Periscope*, April 29, 2018. https://www.pscp.tv/w/1lDGLaBmWRwJm.

[11] Ravikant, Naval. Twitter, Twitter.com/Naval.

[12] Naval Ravikant, "What the World's Smartest People Do When They Want to Get to the Next Level," interview by Adrian Bye, *MeetInnovators*, Adrian Bye, April 1, 2013. http://meetinnovators.com/2013/04/01/naval-ravikant-angellist/.

[13] "Episode 2—Notions of Capital & Naval Ravikant of Angellist," *Origins* from SoundCloud. https://soundcloud.com/notation-capital.

[14] "Naval Ravikant—A Monk in Silicon Valley Tells Us He's Ruthless About Time." *Outliers with Panjak Mishra* from Soundcloud, 2017. https://soundcloud.com/factordaily/ep-06-naval-ravikant-angellis.

[15] Ravikant, Naval and Babak Nivi. "Before Product-Market Fit, Find Passion-Market Fit." *Venture Hacks,* July 17, 2011. https://venturehacks.com/articles/passion-market.

[16] Cohan, Peter. "AngelList: How a Silicon Valley Mogul Found His Passion." *Forbes*, February 6, 2012. https://www.forbes.com/sites/petercohan/2012/02/06/angellist-how-a-silicon-valley-mogul-found-his-passion/#78202c97bbe6.

[17] Ravikant, Naval. "Why You Can't Hire." *Naval*, December 13, 2011. https://startupboy.com/2011/12/13/why-you-cant-hire/.

[18] Ravikant, Naval. "The Returns to Entrepreneurship." *Naval*, November 9, 2009. https://startupboy.com/2009/11/09/the-returns-to-entrepreneurship/.

[19] Ravikant, Naval. "Build a Team That Ships." *Naval*, April 27, 2012. https://startupboy.com/2012/04/27/build-a-team-that-ships/.

[20] Ravikant, Naval. "The 80-Hour Myth." *Naval*, November 29, 2005. https://startupboy.com/2005/11/29/the-80-hour-myth/.

[21] Ravikant, Naval. "The Unbundling of the Venture Capital Industry." *Naval*, December 1, 2010. https://startupboy.com/2010/12/01/the-unbundling-of-the-venture-capital-industry/.

[22] Ravikant, Naval. "Funding Markets Develop in Reverse." *Naval*, December 1, 2010. https://startupboy.com/2010/12/01/funding-markets-develop-in-reverse/.

[23] Nivi, Babak. "Startups Are Here to Save the World." *Venture Hacks,* February 7, 2013. https://venturehacks.com/articles/save-the-world.

[24] Nivi, Babak. "The Entrepreneurial Age." *Venture Hacks,* February 25, 2013. https://venturehacks.com/articles/the-entrepreneurial-age.

[25] Ravikant, Naval. "VC Bundling." *Naval*, December 1, 2005. https://startupboy.com/2005/12/01/vc-bundling/.

[26] Ravikant, Naval. "A Venture SLA." *Naval,* June 28, 2013. https://startupboy.com/2013/06/28/a-venture-sla/.

[27] Nivi, Babak. "No Tradeoff between Quality and Scale." *Venture Hacks*, February 18, 2013. https://venturehacks.com/there-is-no-finish-line-for-entrepreneurs.

[30] Ravikant, Naval, "An interview with Naval Ravikant," interview by Elad Gil, *High Growth Handbook,* Stripe Press, 2019. http://growth.eladgil.com/book/cofounders/managing-your-board-an-interview-with-naval-ravikant-part-1/.

[31] Ferriss, Tim. "Tools of Titans—A Few Goodies from the Cutting Room Floor." *The Tim Ferriss Show,* June 20, 2017. https://tim.blog/2017/06/20/tools-of-titans-goodies/.

[32] Delevett, Peter. "Naval Ravikant of AngelList Went from Dot-Com Pariah to Silicon Valley Power Broker." *The Mercury News,* February 6, 2013. https://www.mercurynews.com/2013/02/06/naval-ravikant-of-angellist-went-from-dot-com-pariah-to-silicon-valley-power-broker/.

[33] Coburn, Lawrence. "The Quiet Rise of AngelList." *The Next Web*, October 4, 2010. https://thenextweb.com/location/2010/10/04/the-quiet-rise-of-angellist/.

[34] Loizos, Conny. "His Brand Burnished, Naval Ravikant Plans New Fund with Babak Nivi." *The PEHub Network*, November 5, 2010.

[35] Nivi, Babak. "Venture Hacks Sucks Now, All You Talk About Is AngelList." *Venture Hacks,* February 17, 2011, https://venturehacks.com/articles/venture-hacks-sucks.

[36] Kincaid, Jason. "The Venture Hacks Startup List Helps Fledgling Startups Pitch Top Angel Investors." *TechCrunch,* February 3 2010. https://techcrunch.com/2010/02/03/startuplist-angel-investors/.

[37] Babak, Nivi. "1.5 Years of AngelList: 8000 Intros, 400 Investments, and That's Just the Data We Can Tell You About." *Venture Hacks*, July 25, 2011. https://venturehacks.com/articles/centi-sesquicentennial.

[38] Smillie, Eric. "Avenging Angel." *Dartmouth Alumni Magazine*, Winter 2014. https://dartmouthalumnimagazine.com/articles/avenging-angel.

[39] Babak, Nivi. "AngelList New Employee Reading List." *Venture Hacks*, October 26, 2013. https://venturehacks.com/articles/reading.

[40] Babak, Nivi. "Things We Care About at AngelList." *Venture Hacks*, October 11, 2013. http://venturehacks.com/articles/care.

[41] Rivlin, Gary. "Founders of Web Site Accuse Backers of Cheating Them." *The New York Times*, January 26, 2005. https://www.nytimes.com/2005/01/26/technology/founders-of-web-site-accuse-backers-of-cheating-them.html.

[42] PandoDaily. "PandoMonthly: Fireside Chat with AngelList Co-Founder Naval Ravikant." November 17, 2012. YouTube video, 2:03:52. https://www.youtube.com/watch?v=2htl-O1oDcI.

[43] Ravikant, Naval. "Ep. 30—Naval Ravikant—AngelList (1 of 2)." Interview by Kevin Weeks. *Venture Studio*, 2016.

[44] Sloan, Paul. "AngelList Attacks Another Startup Pain Point: Legal Fees." CNet, September 5, 2012. https://www.cnet.com/news/angellist-attacks-another-startup-pain-point-legal-fees/.

[45] Ravikant, Naval. "Naval Ravikant on How Crypto Is Squeezing VCs, Hindering Regulators, and Bringing Users Choice." Interview by Laura Shin. *UnChained*, November 29, 2017. http://unchainedpodcast.co/naval-ravikant-on-how-crypto-is-squeezing-vcs-hindering-regulators-and-bringing-users-choice.

[46] Ravikant, Naval. "Introducing: Venture Hacks." *Naval*, April 2, 2007. https://startupboy.com/2007/04/02/introducing-venture-hacks/.

[47] Ravikant, Naval. "Ep. 31—Naval Ravikant—AngelList (2 of 2)." Interview by Kevin Weeks. *Venture Studio*, 2016.

[48] AngelList. "Syndicates/For Investors." https://angel.co/syndicates/for-investors#syndicates.

[49] Ferriss, Tim. "You'd Like to Be an Angel Investor? Here's How You Can Invest in My Deals..." *The Tim Ferriss Show,* September 23, 2013. https://tim.blog/2013/09/23/youd-like-to-be-an-angel-investor-heres-how-you-can-invest-in-my-deals/.

[50] Buhr, Sarah. "AngelList Acquires Product Hunt." *TechCrunch,* December 1, 2016. https://techcrunch.com/2016/12/01/angelhunt/.

[51] Wagner, Kurt. "AngelList Has Acquired Product Hunt for around $20 Million." *Vox*, December 1, 2016. https://www.recode.net/2016/12/1/13802154/angellist-product-hunt-acquisition.

[52] Hoover, Ryan. "Connect the Dots." *Ryan Hoover,* May 1, 2013. http://ryanhoover.me/post/49363486516/connect-the-dots.

[53] "Naval Ravikant." *Angel*. https://angel.co/naval.

[54] Babak, Nivi. "Welcoming the Kauffman Foundation." *Venture Hacks,* October 5, 2010. http://venturehacks.com/articles/kauffman.

[55] "Introducing CoinList." *Medium,* October 20, 2017. https://medium.com/@coinlist/introducing-coinlist-16253eb5cdc3.

[56] Hochstein, Marc. "Most Influential in Blockchain 2017 #4: Naval Ravikant." *CoinDesk*, December 31, 2017. https://www.coindesk.com/coindesk-most-influential-2017-4-naval-ravikant/.

[57] Henry, Zoe. "Why a Group of AngelList and Uber Expats Launched This New Crowdfunding Website." *Inc.*, July 18, 2016. https://www.inc.com/zoe-henry/republic-launches-with-angellist-and-uber-alumni.html.

[58] "New Impact, New Inclusion in Equity Crowdfunding." *Republic,* July 18, 2016. https://republic.co/blog/new-impact-new-inclusion-in-equity-crowdfunding.

[59] AngelList. "Done Deals." https://angel.co/done-deals.

[60] Ravikant, Naval. "Bitcoin—the Internet of Money." *Naval*, November 7, 2013. https://startupboy.com/2013/11/07/bitcoin-the-internet-of-money/.

[61] Token Summit. "Token Summit II—Cryptocurrency, Money, and the Future with Naval Ravikant." December 22, 2017. YouTube video , 32:47. https://www.youtube.com/watch?v=few99D5WnRg.

[62] Blockstreet HQ. "Beyond Blockchain Episode #3: Naval Ravikant." December 5, 2018. YouTube video, 6:01. https://www.youtube.com/watch?v=jCtOHUMaUY8.

[63] Ravikant, Naval. "The Truth About Hard Work." *Naval*, December 25, 2018. https://startupboy.com/2018/12/25/the-truth-about-hard-work/.

[64] "Live Stories: The Present and Future of Crypto with Naval Ravikant and Balaji Srinivasan." *Listen Notes*, November 16, 2018.

[65] Blockstack. "Investment Panel: Naval Ravikant, Meltem Demirors, Garry Tan." August 11, 2017. YouTube video, 27:16. https://www.youtube.com/watch?v=o1mkxci6vvo.

[66] Yang, Sizhao (@zaoyang). "1/Why Does the ICO Opportunity Exist at All?" August 19, 2017, 1:43 p.m. https://twitter.com/zaoyang/status/899008960220372992.

[67] Ravikant, Naval. "Towards a Literate Nation." *Naval*, December 11, 2011. https://startupboy.com/2011/12/11/towards-a-literate-nation/.

[68] Ravikant, Naval. "Be Chaotic Neutral." *Naval*, October 31, 2006. https://startupboy.com/2006/10/31/be-chaotic-neutral/.

[69] AngelList. "AngelList Year in Review." 2018. https://angel.co/2018.

[70] Ravikant, Naval. "The Fifth Protocol." *Naval*, April 1, 2014. https://startupboy.com/2014/04/01/the-fifth-protocol/.

[71] "Is Naval the Ravikant the Nicest Guy in Tech?" *Product Hunt*, September 21, 2015. https://blog.producthunt.com/is-naval-ravikant-the-nicest-guy-in-tech-7f5261d1c23c.

[72] Ravikant, Naval. "Life Formulas I." *Naval,* February 8, 2008. https://startupboy.com/2008/02/08/life-formulas-i/.

[73] @ScottAdamsSays. "Scott Adams Talks to Naval..." *Periscope,* 2018. https://www.pscp.tv/w/1nAKERdZMkkGL.

[74] @Naval. "Naval Ravikant was live." *Periscope*, February 2019. https://www.pscp.tv/w/1nAKEyeLYmRKL.

[75] "4 Kinds of Luck." https://nav.al/money-luck.

[76] Kaiser, Caleb. "Naval Ravikant's Guide to Choosing Your First Job in Tech." *AngelList,* February 21, 2019. https://angel.co/blog/naval-ravikants-guide-to-choosing-your-first-job-in-tech?utm_campaign=platform-newsletter&utm_medium=email.

[77] PowerfulJRE. "Joe Rogan Experience #1309—Naval Ravikant." June 4, 2019. YouTube video, 2:11:56. https://www.youtube.com/watch?v=3qHkcs3kG44.

[78] Ravikant, Naval. "How to Get Rich: Every Episode." *Naval,* June 3, 2019. https://nav.al/how-to-get-rich.

[79] Ravikant, Naval. Original content created for this book, September 2019.

[80] Jorgenson, Eric. Original content written for this book, June 2019.

I ABOUT THE AUTHOR

ERIC JORGENSON is a product strategist and writer. In 2011, he joined the founding team of Zaarly, a company dedicated to helping homeowners find accountable service providers they can trust. His business blog, *Evergreen*, educates and entertains more than one million readers.

Eric is on a quest to create—and eat—the perfect sandwich. He lives in Kansas City with Jeannine, the most wonderful woman in the world. Follow him on Twitter @ericjorgenson, or check out his new projects on ejorgenson.com.